*Life Writing* offers the novice writer engaging and creative activities, making use of insightful, relevant readings from well-known authors to illustrate the techniques presented. This volume makes use of new versions of key chapters from the recent Routledge/Open University text-book, *Creative Writing: A Workbook with Readings* for writers who are specialising in life writing.

Using their experience and expertise as teachers as well as authors, Derek Neale and Sara Haslam guide aspiring writers through such key writing skills as:

- writing what you know
- investigating biography and autobiography
- using prefaces
- finding a form
- using memory
- developing characters
- using novelistic, poetic and dramatic techniques.

The volume is further updated to include never-before published interviews and conversations with successful life writers such as Jenny Diski, Robert Fraser, Richard Holmes, Michael Holroyd, Jackie Kay, Hanif Kureishi and Blake Morrison. Concise and practical, *Life Writing* offers an inspirational guide to the methods and techniques of authorship and is a must-read for aspiring writers.

**Sara Haslam** is Lecturer in Literature at the Open University. She is the author of *Fragmenting Modernism: Ford Madox Ford, the Novel and the Great War* (2002), and editor of Ford's *England and the English* (2003) as well as *Ford Madox Ford and the City* (2005). She is working on a study of Ford's biography.

**Derek Neale** is Lecturer in Creative Writing at the Open University. He is an award winning fiction writer and much of his PhD research focused on the link between writing and memory. He is editor and co-author of *A Creative Writing Handbook* (2009) and co-author of *Writing Fiction* (2008, Routledge).

# RELATED TITLES FROM ROUTLEDGE AND THE OPEN UNIVERSITY

## Writing Fiction
*Sara Haslam and Derek Neale*

This useful volume guides aspiring writers through crucial aspects of their craft, outlining how to stimulate creativity, keeping a writer's notebook, character creation, setting, point of view, structure and showing and telling. *Writing Fiction* includes never-before published interviews with writers such as Andrew Cowan, Stevie Davies, Maggie Gee, Andrew Greig and Hanif Kureishi.

ISBN13: 978–0–415–46155–9 (pbk)
December 2008

## Writing Poetry
*Bill Herbert*

Concise and highly useful, *Writing Poetry* offers a clearly written, inspirational guide to methods and techniques of poetry, covering drafting, line, voice, imagery, rhyme, form and theme. This volume presents never-before published interviews with poets such as Vicki Feaver, Douglas Dunn, Gillian Allnutt, Jo Shapcott, Kathleen Jamie, Linda France and Sean O'Brien.

ISBN13: 978–0–415–46154–2 (pbk)
July 2009

Available at all good bookshops
For ordering and further information please visit:
www.routledgeliterature.com

# Life Writing

*Sara Haslam and Derek Neale*

Routledge
Taylor & Francis Group

LONDON AND NEW YORK

First edition published 2009
by Routledge
2 Park Square, Milton Park, Abingdon, Oxon, OX14 4RN

Simultaneously published in the USA and Canada
by Routledge
270 Madison Ave, New York, NY 10016

*Routledge is an imprint of the Taylor & Francis Group, an informa business*

© 2009 Sara Haslam and Derek Neale

Typeset in Frutiger and Times by RefineCatch Limited, Bungay, Suffolk
Printed and bound in Great Britain by TJ International Ltd, Padstow, Cornwall

*British Library Cataloguing in Publication Data*
A catalogue record for this book is available from the British Library

*Library of Congress Cataloging-in-Publication Data*
Haslam, Sara.
Life writing / Sara Haslam and Derek Neale.—1st ed.
p. cm.
Includes bibliographical references and index.
1. Creative writing (Higher education)—Problems, exercises, etc.
2. English language—Rhetoric—Study and teaching.
3. Authorship—Problems, exercises, etc.
I. Neale, Derek. II. Title.
PE1404.H384 2008
808'.042076—dc22
2008028830

ISBN13: 978–0–415–46153–5
ISBN10: 0–415–46153–7

# Contents

# Acknowledgements

The publisher and authors would like to thank the following for permission to reprint material under copyright:

'Death of a Naturalist' from Seamus Heaney (1980) *Selected Poems 1965–1975*, London: Faber and Faber Ltd. Copyright © 1980 by Seamus Heaney. Reproduced by permission of Faber and Faber Ltd.

Excerpt from Laurie Lee (1962) *Cider with Rosie*, Harmondsworth: Penguin. Copyright © 1959 by Laurie Lee. Reproduced by permission of PFD (www.pfd.co.uk) on behalf of Laurie Lee.

Extract from Lesley Glaister, 'Memory: The Key to Real Imagining', from Julia Bell and Paul Magrs (eds) (2001) *The Creative Writing Coursebook*, London: Macmillan. Copyright © by Lesley Glaister. Reprinted by permission of A.M. Heath & Co Ltd.

Extracts from Hilary Mantel (2003) *Giving up the Ghost: A Memoir*, London: Fourth Estate. Copyright © 2003 by Hilary Mantel. Reprinted by permission of HarperCollins Publishers Ltd, and of A.M. Heath & Co Ltd.

Extract from Anne Frank (1997) *The Diary of a Young Girl: The Definitive Edition* (Otto H. Frank and Mirjam Pressler (eds), Susan Massotty (trans.)), London: Viking, 1997. Copyright © 1991 by The Anne Frank-Fonds, Basle, Switzerland. English translation copyright © 1995 by Doubleday a division of Bantam Doubleday Dell Publishing Group Inc. Reproduced by permission of Penguin Books Ltd, of Doubleday, a division of Random House, Inc., and of Liepman AG, Zurich.

Extract from 'To the Tempest Given', by Richard Holmes (2000) *Sidetracks: Explorations of a romantic biographer*, London: HarperCollins. Copyright © 2000 by Richard Holmes. Reprinted by permission of David Godwin Associates Ltd. on behalf of Richard Holmes.

Extract from 'I Always Wanted You to Admire My Fasting; or, Looking at Kafka', from Philip Roth (1975) *Reading Myself and Others*, London: Jonathan Cape. Copyright © 1969, 1975 by Philip Roth. Reprinted by permission of Farrar, Straus and Giroux, and of The Random House Group Ltd.

'Parents' Day' from Sharon Olds (1996) *The Wellspring*, London: Jonathan Cape. Copyright © 1996 by Sharon Olds. Reprinted by permission of Alfred A. Knopf, a division of The Random House Group Ltd.

Extract from Joan Didion (2003) *Where I Was From*, London: Flamingo. Copyright © 2003 by Joan Didion. Reprinted by permission of HarperCollins Publishers Ltd.

'Long Distance' from Tony Harrison (1984) *Tony Harrison: Selected Poems*, London: Penguin. Copyright © 1984, 1987 by Tony Harrison. Reproduced by kind permission of the author.

Extract from Richard Holmes (1985) *Footsteps: Adventures of a Romantic Biographer*, London: Flamingo. Copyright © 1985 by Richard Holmes. Reproduced by permission of HarperCollins Publishers Limited.

Extract from Dervla Murphy (1968) *In Ethiopia with a Mule*, London: John Murray. Reproduced by kind permission of the author.

Extracts from Lorna Sage (2000) *Bad Blood: A Memoir*, London: Fourth Estate. Copyright © 2000 by Lorna Sage. Reprinted by permission of HarperCollins Publishers Ltd.

Extract from Wole Soyinka (1991) *Aké: The Years of Childhood*, London: Methuen Publishing Ltd. Reproduced by permission of The Random House Group Ltd.

Extract from David Jenkins with Sue Rogers (1993) *Richard Burton: A Brother Remembered*, London: Century. Reprinted by permission of The Random House Group Ltd and Elspeth Cochrane Personal Management.

'Fifth Philosopher's Song' from Aldous Huxley (1962) *Collected Poetry of Aldous Huxley*. Copyright © 1962, 1970 by Aldous Huxley. Reprinted by permission of Georges Borchardt Inc. for the estate of Aldous Huxley.

Extract from John Diamond (1998) *C: Because Cowards Get Cancer Too*, London: Vermilion. Reprinted by permission of The Random House Group Ltd.

Extract from George Alagiah (2002) *A Passage to Africa*, London: Time Warner Books. Copyright © 2001 by George Alagiah. Reproduced by kind permission of Little, Brown Book Group Ltd, and of the author, care of The Hanbury Agency, 28 Moreton Street, London SW1V 2PE.

Extract from Nigel Nicolson, *Portrait of a Marriage*, London: Weidenfeld & Nicolson, a division of The Orion Publishing Group. Copyright © 1973 by Nigel Nicolson: All rights reserved. Reproduced by permission of The Orion Publishing Group, and of Scribner, an imprint of Simon & Schuster Adult Publishing Group.

'Preface' from Mark Lewisohn (2002) *Funny Peculiar – The True Story of Benny Hill*, London: PanMacmillan. Copyright © 2002 by Mark Lewisohn. Reproduced with permission of the publisher.

Extract from John Bayley (1998) *Iris: A Memoir of Iris Murdoch*, London: Duckworth. Reprinted by permission of Gerald Duckworth & Co. Ltd.

Extract from Gillian Slovo (1997) *Every Secret Thing*, London: Abacus. Copyright © 1997 by Gillian Slovo. Reprinted by permission of Little, Brown & Company.

Selection from 'Epilogue: "In December 1991 my daughter, Paula . . . swimming with plans for greatness"', from Isabel Allende (1994) *Paula* (Margaret Sayers Peden, trans.), London: Flamingo. Copyright © 1994 by Isabel Allende, translation copyright © 1995 by HarperCollins Publishers. Reprinted by permission of HarperCollins Publishers Ltd, and of Agencia Literaria Carmen Balcells S.A.

Extract from Pete Hamill (1995) *A Drinking Life: A memoir*, London: Little, Brown & Co. Copyright © 1993 by Pete Hamill. Reprinted by permission of Little, Brown & Co, and of International Creative Management, Inc.

'Calliope in the labour ward', 'Song of power' and 'Marriage' from Elaine Feinstein (2002) *Collected Poems and Translations*, Manchester: Carcanet

# Introduction

## Sara Haslam and Derek Neale

The subject of this book is 'life writing', an umbrella term for biography and autobiography, which also covers popular sub-genres – like travel writing, for example.

Late in the seventeenth century, the poet and dramatist John Dryden defined biography as the 'history of particular men's lives'. Now we would qualify his definition with the inclusion of women's lives (biographies of Madonna and Diana, Princess of Wales, outsell those of Dryden!). In this age of celebrity, interpretation of the word 'particular' might well also be different from Dryden's. But readers still expect a biography – and an autobiography – to give an account of a person's life and times.

*Life Writing* is the work of two authors who have produced and run popular and successful creative writing courses for the Open University. We have also taught writing and literature at the University of Chester, King's College London and the University of East Anglia, the latter an institution which pioneered the teaching of creative writing in British higher education and which is a famous producer of published writers.

*Life Writing* features new versions of chapters from our acclaimed Open University course book, *Creative Writing: A Workbook with Readings*, which is used in many university and college courses and has achieved worldwide sales. We have revised the chapters specialising in life writing to integrate short illustrative readings. We have also incorporated interviews and conversations with contemporary practitioners. Writers such as Jenny Diski, Richard Holmes, Michael Holroyd, Jackie Kay, Hanif Kureishi and Blake Morrison reveal how they regard working with personal memories, what they see as the difference between biography and autobiography, and how they utilise fictional techniques in their life writing.

This is a highly practical book. It is designed to help you generate your own projects. Each chapter contains several writing exercises. Their purpose is to give you immediate practice in the approaches under discussion. These activities are meant to be engaging and enjoyable, provocative and challenging. If you dislike an exercise, try it anyway. Sometimes irritation or resistance can prove to be a surprising creative force. You may find that some of the exercises add more than just new approaches to your writing toolkit. You may come up with the seed of a narrative, some personal memory or observation about a life that you can use in a new way. If you enjoy a particular exercise, you may want to devote more time to it or return to it and try out variations. Most of the exercises are designed to take between 15–60 minutes, but if you find yourself working on an exercise for hours, rejoice – the exercise is on its way to becoming something more.

Throughout this book, we investigate how biography and autobiography are generated and crafted and how creativity and imagination are as crucial to the life writing project as they are to other more likely genres such as fiction, poetry and drama. We explore how lives might be seen to be stories, and the best ways of retelling those stories. A series of examples illuminate how other writers have embraced the challenge of writing about a life. We introduce a wide range of techniques to enable you to make best use of your memory and imagination, to help transform factual information into something worth reading, as well as suggesting methods to help you undertake and incorporate appropriate research in your projects. We see keeping a writer's notebook as a key tool, enabling you to treat writing as a habit. If you haven't got a notebook already we advise you to go out and get one early on, as you begin working your way through the chapters. Your notebook is where you can store observations, responses to what you read and your writing experiments – it acts as a repository and a spur, sparking your memory, imagination and commitment.

*Life Writing* is appropriate for use on courses as part of workshop teaching, by writers' groups, or by individual writers working alone. It

Now look at your surroundings and write a paragraph (no more than 150 words) describing them, picking out at least three things that you haven't noticed recently – things you didn't think of when you closed your eyes.

### *Discussion*

The details you noticed may have come in various guises. You may have seen some dirt on the floor, something that isn't usually there. You may have noticed an ornament that you haven't looked at for a while, an object that's always present but not always seen. You may have picked up on the colour of a wall, the handle on a door. Some of these things will have changed since the last time you noticed them – maybe the wall colour has faded. Some things will not be quite as you thought they were – maybe you didn't remember the door handle being made of metal. It is useful to do this sort of perceptual exercise at regular intervals. In this way you will revive the way you see the world – by de-familiarising your perceptions you will reinvigorate your writing.

Here are some similar follow-up exercises that you can try when you get time.

Try the same exercise on a different, but still familiar, place. You can also try it with familiar characters in your life – describe them in their absence and then take note of the things you didn't recall.

Think of the details of a short journey – say to the shops, to work or even to another part of your home – a journey that you make regularly. Jot these details down. Now make the journey, making a point of looking for things that you haven't noticed recently. Write a paragraph about the journey using the new details.

Write a paragraph describing a simple action that you do every day – for example, washing, cooking, shaving, putting on make-up, feeding the cat. When you next perform the action, notice everything about it and afterwards note down details that weren't in your original paragraph.

### *Collecting and selecting*

Use your notebook to gather observations about your environment. It is important to go about your daily business with your eyes open and all your other senses similarly alert. Accumulate details about the world around you. For instance, using an imaginary scenario, you might notice how the man along the road twitches his curtains, how he wears colour co-ordinated clothes, usually but not always green. Note the melancholic tone of his voice and how he goes to the post office every Monday at 9.30 am, accompanied by his neighbour who often wears a purple sari. You might note how they walk faster as they pass the graffiti on the factory wall and often smile at the 'Elvis lives' slogan that someone has daubed on the adjoining wall. You might note how, at the post office, they both chat to a man with a white Scottie, a dog who snarls at most passers-by when he is tied to the railings outside the shop, but not at the man and his neighbour.

By noting such details you are collecting materials that you might use later in your writing. In the imaginary scenario above, we have almost formed a narrative. At times you might do this, at other times you might be more arbitrary and fragmented in what you gather, writing down a range of dissimilar observations: the weather, a character description, an overheard turn of phrase. You don't need to make complete sentences or connect it all into a sequence; you could make a list of bullet points. In whatever form, collecting serves to revive a certain detailed way of seeing the world: how you might have grasped the world as a child.

Perception is always a selective faculty. You will not be able to see all and everything anew each and every day. However, you can use tactics to keep yourself alert: cross over the road and walk on a different side, or sit in a chair that you don't usually use. It is important to develop an investigative attitude to your own environment, to look at things from a slightly different angle, and to search for the previously unnoticed. Eventually, when coming to write, you will realise that, like perception, writing is also selective. You will pick the details to be included and excluded: which detail acts as a useful repetition, and which detail might be redundant. You can't pick and choose if you haven't gathered enough information in the first place.

In our scenario above, for instance: the man at the post office with the dog might have fluffy white whiskers just like his white Scottie – this is a relatively significant and amusing detail. The same man might wear a plain-coloured tie, which is less interesting information. Each piece of writing that you work on will demand its own level and type of detail. Details attain significance, for you and consequently for your reader, not just through being dramatic or unusual. Often they will attain significance because they are being noticed for the first time, because a may be worked through sequentially or used as a resource book for both writers and writing tutors to dip into as needed. If you are a writer working on your own, you may wonder how to gauge the effectiveness of your writings. The discussion sections after each activity give guidance on how to review what you've done.

We start by exploring some of the ways in which, as writers, we can make use of the world around us, transforming the material immediately at hand, and also that which is further out of reach.

# Writing what you know

*Derek Neale*

Creative writing courses and manuals often offer the advice 'write what you know'. This is undoubtedly good advice, yet what exactly does it mean? Many writers testify to using their life experiences – their memories and their everyday perceptions – as a source for their fiction or poetry, as well as for their autobiographies and memoirs. Yet these experiences aren't necessarily extraordinary in themselves. You don't have to have led an unusual or exotic life in order to write. You do, however, need to raise your level of perception above the ordinary. Writing what you know means being aware of your own world, both past and present, in as full a way as possible.

This chapter will introduce and briefly elaborate on some of the ways in which you might 'know' the world around you. By looking at the commonplace details of your life in a different way, using your sensory perceptions and learning to use your own memories, you will be exercising certain writing muscles, ones that need regular flexing. In this way you may discover you know more than you thought.

**Activity 1.1    Writing**

Write down a quick sentence in response to the advice 'write what you know'. What does it immediately suggest to you?

## *Discussion*

You may react positively to such advice; you may be able to go off happily and make use of every last ounce of your life experience, without doubt or consternation. Or you may think: 'I don't know anything'; 'all that I know is boring'; 'nobody would want to know what I know' or 'I know too much, how could I possibly get that down in words?'

Whatever your response, the aim of this chapter is to broaden the meaning of such advice; it should act as a prompt the next time you hear it, reminding you that you have numerous ways of exploiting the raw materials of your own life.

## The everyday

Writing is a perceptual art, one in which images are created via language in order for the reader to make meaning. It is therefore imperative that the writer's powers of perception are alert. Writing is a process of becoming aware, of opening the senses to ways of grasping the world, ways that may previously have been blocked. Often we take the world around us for granted; we are so immersed in habit. All of our lives contain relative degrees of routine. We go to sleep, we eat, we go to work. The things we may choose to write about will also contain repeated and habitual elements. How many times have you come across the word 'usually' in memoirs and biographies, or phrases such as 'every day' and 'every year'? How many times do you read about meals, or other daily routines like journeys to work, meetings with friends? These are only a few of the many designators of habitual patterns of behaviour, giving the impression of life passing in a routine fashion. Taken out of context such details might be uninteresting, but in fact they are invariably the parts of the writing that build a world for the reader. This world is believable because it appears to have existed before the reader started reading about it and will continue on afterwards.

## Activity 1.2   Writing

Close your eyes for a few moments and think of the room or place around you. Think of the details that you would include in any description and make a mental note of them. Open your eyes and, without looking around, write down what you thought of.

Now look at your surroundings and write a paragraph (no more than 150 words) describing them, picking out at least three things that you haven't noticed recently – things you didn't think of when you closed your eyes.

The details you noticed may have come in various guises. You may have seen some dirt on the floor, something that isn't usually there. You may have noticed an ornament that you haven't looked at for a while, an object that's always present but not always seen. You may have picked up on the colour of a wall, the handle on a door. Some of these things will have changed since the last time you noticed them – maybe the wall colour has faded. Some things will not be quite as you thought they were – maybe you didn't remember the door handle being made of metal. It is useful to do this sort of perceptual exercise at regular intervals. In this way you will revive the way you see the world – by de-familiarising your perceptions you will reinvigorate your writing.

Here are some similar follow-up exercises that you can try when you get time.

Try the same exercise on a different, but still familiar, place. You can also try it with familiar characters in your life – describe them in their absence and then take note of the things you didn't recall.

Think of the details of a short journey – say to the shops, to work or even to another part of your home – a journey that you make regularly. Jot these details down. Now make the journey, making a point of looking for things that you haven't noticed recently. Write a paragraph about the journey using the new details.

Write a paragraph describing a simple action that you do every day – for example, washing, cooking, shaving, putting on make-up, feeding the cat. When you next perform the action, notice everything about it and afterwards note down details that weren't in your original paragraph.

### *Collecting and selecting*

Use your notebook to gather observations about your environment. It is important to go about your daily business with your eyes open and all your other senses similarly alert. Accumulate details about the world around you. For instance, using an imaginary scenario, you might notice how the man along the road twitches his curtains, how he wears colour co-ordinated clothes, usually but not always green. Note the melancholic tone of his voice and how he goes to the post office every Monday at 9.30 am, accompanied by his neighbour who often wears a purple sari. You might note how they walk faster as they pass the graffiti on the factory wall and often smile at the 'Elvis lives' slogan that someone has daubed on the adjoining wall. You might note how, at the post office, they both chat to a man with a white Scottie, a dog who snarls at most passers-by when he is tied to the railings outside the shop, but not at the man and his neighbour.

By noting such details you are collecting materials that you might use later in your writing. In the imaginary scenario above, we have almost formed a narrative. At times you might do this, at other times you might be more arbitrary and fragmented in what you gather, writing down a range of dissimilar observations: the weather, a character description, an overheard turn of phrase. You don't need to make complete sentences or connect it all into a sequence; you could make a list of bullet points. In whatever form, collecting serves to revive a certain detailed way of seeing the world: how you might have grasped the world as a child.

Perception is always a selective faculty. You will not be able to see all and everything anew each and every day. However, you can use tactics to keep yourself alert: cross over the road and walk on a different side, or sit in a chair that you don't usually use. It is important to develop an investigative attitude to your own environment, to look at things from a slightly different angle, and to search for the previously unnoticed. Eventually, when coming to write, you will realise that, like perception, writing is also selective. You will pick the details to be included and excluded: which detail acts as a useful repetition, and which detail might be redundant. You can't pick and choose if you haven't gathered enough information in the first place.

In our scenario above, for instance: the man at the post office with the dog might have fluffy white whiskers just like his white Scottie – this is a relatively significant and amusing detail. The same man might wear a plain-coloured tie, which is less interesting information. Each piece of writing that you work on will demand its own level and type of detail. Details attain significance, for you and consequently for your reader, not just through being dramatic or unusual. Often they will attain significance because they are being noticed for the first time, because a usual or habitual perception has shifted. For instance, returning to the scenario above, every day you might walk past the graffiti on the wall, considering it to be an inane and messy scrawl, if you notice it at all. Then one day you see a sunrise painted behind the letters, or you might see 'Elvis lives' and realise for the first time that these words are anagrams, or that the yellow lettering matches the colour of the bedding flowers just planted by the council, or you might have a flashback of the bare concrete behind the graffiti and what the wall used to be like. It is these shifts in the way you see your familiar world that revive it. In this way writing is a process of scrutinising, looking closely at things, and then taking the observations onto a new level of perception, one in which you understand your world just a little more.

Some of the observational detail collected in your notebook might seem mundane and indiscriminate, its interest and significance not fully known even to you. Some of it might be more focused on something you are working on – an observation of a certain place or type of place. For instance, you may be writing about a childhood incident at a swimming pool and need to remind yourself of the smell of chlorine and the strange acoustics. Whether apparently insignificant or more focused, there is no prescription for the sort of observations you should make; they will always be personal to the individual writer.

### *Using your observations*

The observations you make in your notebook might not always appear imaginative or pertinent to anything, but the mundane recording of events may have unlikely uses. Writing in my notebook on 15 December 1998, I observed the sky – at the coast on a murky winter's day, when the low cloud seemed to be lit by a churning, subterranean force:

> the earth comes to the surface, the soil muddies the sky, clouds the air – it even turns the sea into a sandy mix . . . the sea, the puddles, the rivers, the sky – all glow brown, glisten, shimmer – but not with the light of any sun.

On another occasion in the same notebook I observed a familiar river, and how the current flowed in 'one concerted way in the straights but was torn between two directions at the bends'. By struggling to express what I saw on those two separate days, the observations stayed with me. What you put down in your notebook can act as a mnemonic, a memory aid, reminding you of the original observation, reviving certain thoughts and emotions. In this way your notebook – as well as being a writing 'gym' where you exercise perceptual and linguistic muscles – can also act as a future resource.

## The senses

Becoming more aware of the everyday world around you involves more than just looking. If writing is a perceptual art then perception should involve all of the senses, not just the visual. You must also start to smell, feel, taste and hear the world you are trying to realise. So, in the made up scenario, when you see the man with the Scottie dog you might be too fearful to stroke his dog, but perhaps you could touch the cold metal bar where the dog was tied up – after he is gone, of course! You might feel the rough bark of the tree close at hand, smell the brash perfume of the washing detergent steaming out of the nearby launderette, taste the bitter dryness this causes in your mouth, and hear the wind whistle past the buildings. You might see the graffiti on the wall and appreciate that part of the street is always quiet, not even any traffic, and that there is a different smell: ammonia, it smells like fish.

By awakening your senses and becoming more conscious of the world around you, you will be enriching your grasp of that world. Once this heightened way of perceiving your environment has trickled down into your writing, your reader will benefit, getting a much fuller picture of the worlds you are writing about.

## Activity 1.3   Writing and Research

In an indoor location write down three things for each of the following:

- sounds that you can hear;
- textures that you can feel;
- odours that you can smell;
- flavours that you can taste;
- objects that you can see.

These sensory perceptions will be used again in the next chapter, so make sure you know where to find them in your notebook.

### *Discussion*

Having the sensory perception is one thing; writing about it is quite a different matter. We often need to use metaphor and simile to describe our perceptions. Even the most established writer struggles and strives to find phrases that can translate perception in an original and meaningful fashion. How do you write about feeling 'soaked to the skin' without using such a hackneyed phrase? How do you write about a rough surface or a bitter taste? The obvious solution is to find a comparison that fits the sensation. The rough surface becomes 'like gravel' or 'like sandpaper', the bitter taste becomes 'like lemon'. Some similes might seem a little too easy or too familiar and it is important to search for the metaphor or simile that fits your particular context.

Your writing will always benefit from exercising your sensory awareness. You can do more of these sorts of exercises, and in a variety of contexts. You might like to repeat this activity, finding three of each of the senses in an outdoor location. Also, looking back over and revising your writing should become a habit. Review your responses to Activity 1.3 and check for the sensory perceptions that you have used, add some relevant ones if you need to and redraft accordingly.

### *Contexts*

On their own, sensory perceptions don't tend to mean that much. They depend on a context in which they can be brought to life: for instance, that of a character. Such sensory perceptions as you've just listed in Activity 1.3 might hold more meaning if the man who twitches the curtains was the character smelling the smells or touching the surfaces; if his neighbour in the purple sari was the character hearing the noises, tasting the flavours. Sensory perceptions offer dimensions that will enrich your writing, but generally they cannot operate in isolation.

### Activity 1.4   Reading

Read Seamus Heaney's 'Death of a Naturalist' below and the opening of Laurie Lee's *Cider with Rosie* which follows. Think about the following questions:

- Which sensory perceptions are used, and how are they used?
- Do the perceptions belong to a character?
- Is a place realised through the sensory perceptions?
- How is time being organised?
- Are the perceptions from one moment or many?

### Death of a Naturalist

All year the flax-dam festered in the heart
Of the townland; green and heavy headed
Flax had rotted there, weighted down by huge sods.
Daily it sweltered in the punishing sun.
Bubbles gargled delicately, bluebottles
Wove a strong gauze of sound around the smell.
There were dragon-flies, spotted butterflies,
But best of all was the warm thick slobber
Of frogspawn that grew like clotted water
In the shade of the banks. Here, every spring
I would fill jampotfuls of the jellied
Specks to range on window-sills at home,
On shelves at school, and wait and watch until
The fattening dots burst into nimble-
Swimming tadpoles. Miss Walls would tell us how
The daddy frog was called a bullfrog
And how he croaked and how the mammy frog
Laid hundreds of little eggs and this was
Frogspawn. You could tell the weather by frogs too
For they were yellow in the sun and brown
In rain.

Then one hot day when fields were rank
With cowdung in the grass the angry frogs
Invaded the flax-dam; I ducked through hedges
To a coarse croaking that I had not heard
Before. The air was thick with a bass chorus.
Right down the dam gross-bellied frogs were cocked
On sods; their loose necks pulsed like sails. Some hopped:
The slap and plop were obscene threats. Some sat
Poised like mud grenades, their blunt heads farting.
I sickened, turned, and ran. The great slime kings

Were gathered there for vengeance and I knew
That if I dipped my hand the spawn would clutch it.
(Seamus Heaney 1980: 12–13)

### from *Cider With Rosie*

I WAS set down from the carrier's cart at the age of three; and there
with a sense of bewilderment and terror my life in the village
began.

The June grass, amongst which I stood, was taller than I was,
and I wept. I had never been so close to grass before. It towered
above me and all around me, each blade tattooed with tiger-skins
of sunlight. It was knife-edged, dark, and a wicked green, thick as
a forest and alive with grasshoppers that chirped and chattered and
leapt through the air like monkeys.

I was lost and didn't know where to move. A tropic heat oozed
up from the ground, rank with sharp odours of roots and nettles.
Snow-clouds of elder-blossom banked in the sky, showering upon
me the fumes and flakes of their sweet and giddy suffocation. High
overhead ran frenzied larks, screaming, as though the sky were
tearing apart.

For the first time in my life I was out of the sight of humans. For
the first time in my life I was alone in a world whose behaviour I
could neither predict nor fathom: a world of birds that squealed,
of plants that stank, of insects that sprang about without warning.
I was lost and I did not expect to be found again. I put back my
head and howled, and the sun hit me smartly on the face, like
a bully.

From this daylight nightmare I was awakened, as from many
another, by the appearance of my sisters. They came scrambling
and calling up the steep rough bank, and parting the long grass
found me. Faces of rose, familiar, living; huge shining faces hung
up like shields between me and the sky; faces with grins and white
teeth (some broken) to be conjured up like genii with a howl,
brushing off terror with their broad scoldings and affection. They
leaned over me one, two, three – their mouths smeared with red
currants and their hands, dripping with juice.

'There, there, it's all right, don't you wail any more. Come down
'ome and we'll stuff you with currants.'

And Marjorie, the eldest, lifted me into her long brown hair, and ran me jogging down the path and through the steep rose-filled garden, and set me down on the cottage doorstep, which was our home, though I couldn't believe it.

That was the day we came to the village, in the summer of the last year of the First World War. To a cottage that stood in a half-acre of garden on a steep bank above a lake; a cottage with three floors and a cellar and a treasure in the walls, with a pump and apple trees, syringa and strawberries, rooks in the chimneys, frogs in the cellar, mushrooms on the ceiling, and all for three and sixpence a week.

I don't know where I lived before then. My life began on the carrier's cart which brought me up the long slow hills to the village, and dumped me in the high grass, and lost me. I had ridden wrapped up in a Union Jack to protect me from the sun, and when I rolled out of it, and stood piping loud among the buzzing jungle of that summer bank, then, I feel, was I born. And to all the rest of us, the whole family of eight, it was the beginning of a life.

(Lee 1962: 9–10).

## Discussion

In 'Death of a Naturalist', notice how the profusion of sensory detail is given the context of a personal memory. This locates it in an activity and place, which gives it significance. In terms of time, notice how the habitual, everyday action is realised in phrases like 'All year'; 'every spring'; 'Miss Walls would tell us how' – and how this is contrasted to the specific time of 'Then one hot day'. In this poem the sensory perception gets so rich and intoxicating that there seems to be some confusion in lines like 'bluebottles/wove a strong gauze of sound around the smell.' The senses (touch, smell, sight and sound) appear to merge. Heaney uses a rhetorical form called 'synaesthesia' – describing one sensory perception according to the terms of another.

Notice in *Cider with Rosie* too that all the senses are activated, and how happily the childlike perception – viewing the world as if for the first time – coincides with Lee's intention: realising this particular world afresh. Amid the flurry of sensory detail there is also a tight organisation of time. Even though Lee's recall of events must be fragmentary and confused, for the purposes of his narrative he has started arranging details in coherent and logical sequence. He is three years old, it is June, he gets deposited from a cart in the grass, feels lost, alone, overwhelmed, and consequently cries, before being rescued by his sisters. In your reading, look out for such temporal organisation, and be similarly aware of it in your own writing.

### Memory and narrative

The philosopher John Locke made the assertion that individual identity is inextricably linked to memory – we are only what we remember being. Memory is a central part of how we think of ourselves, and indeed a central strand of what we might know. Memory is not simply a mechanical process. It works in various ways and you will use it in various ways in your writing. In Chapter 2 you will look at how to make the most of associations that arise from your memories. In Chapter 7, 'Using memory', you will look in more detail at how memory works as a narrative, and how we tell ourselves stories about our own pasts.

Part of what a story does is organise events in time, as Lee has done. Memory often works like this – even when you aren't intending to write your memories down but are simply thinking. So when you try to remember what you did yesterday you start perhaps by recalling some fragments – a conversation, having breakfast, going to the park. The more you think about the fragments, the more you are likely to arrange them in some sort of temporal order – like a story. I had breakfast first, then I went to the park and when I returned, that's when my mother rang. Thinking of memory as a form of narrative or story is a great asset when you come to your own writing. But it's important to consider your memories to be narratives that you can use freely. Don't feel that you have to render them exactly in an 'as it really was' fashion.

### Activity 1.5    Reading

Read the following extract from Lesley Glaister's 'Memory: The true key to real imagining' below. Look for the following things:

- How is the memory realised and written about?
- How is time organised in the memory?
- In Glaister's version of this memory, what really brings it alive?

## from 'Memory: The true key to real imagining'

I am on a beach. I don't know where – Southwold perhaps. I am very small and wearing a blue ruched swimming costume, which scratches the tops of my legs and fills with bubbles of water when I go in the sea. But I'm not in the sea. I'm sitting on a big striped towel, shivering. My dad is sitting beside me and I'm thinking how hairy his legs are, like gorilla's legs. Then I notice something: a hollow in the soft bulge of his calf, big enough to cup an egg in, not hairy like the rest but dull pinkish, fuzzy like newborn mouse skin. I want to put my finger inside and feel but I don't. Somehow I know I can't do that and I must not mention it. Then Dad gets up and hobbles down the shingle towards the sea. He breaks into a run when he gets to the flat bit before the sea begins. He plunges in and swims out and out and out. My mum is reading and my sister shovelling pebbles into a bucket. No one but me has noticed how his head gets smaller and smaller the further out he swims, until at last I can't see him between the waves. He has gone. But I don't shout or scream. I turn over and lie on my tummy on the towel, feeling my heart thudding against the lumpy pebbles. I have seen my daddy drown but I don't say a word. I lie there with the sea or my heart roaring in my ears.

I lie paralysed by fear and guilt for what seems hours until I hear the crunch of footsteps and feel the sprinkle of cold drops on my skin. Daddy is back and is standing above me waiting for me to get off the towel. He is fine, invigorated and oblivious to my terror, rubbing himself dry, slurping tea from the thermos.

That experience encapsulates for me a key moment of growing up: the sudden realization of my dad's vulnerability and his mortality – and by extension that of everyone including myself. An apparently insignificant moment when the bottom fell out of my safe child's world.

It wasn't until my father died, about twenty years later, that the seaside moment came back to me. Only then did it occur to me that the hollow in his leg was the scar of a tropical ulcer contracted during the war. He was one of the soldiers captured by the Japanese when Singapore was taken in 1941. He worked as a slave on the construction of the Burma/Siam railway, suffering cerebral malaria, cholera, dysentery, beatings, near starvation – an unimaginably traumatic time about which he never spoke. It was a deep area of silence. Not only was it never spoken of but there seemed an embargo even on wondering. It wasn't until years after his death that it even occurred to me why, as a naturally curious child, I never even *wondered*.

(Glaister 2001: 75–8.)

### *Discussion*

Notice how the memory is dramatised in the present tense, also how there is a shape to the telling of the memory, as if it were a fictional story with a starting point (father is invincible), a climax (father presumed dead) and a revelation (father is alive but flawed). Also note how the mix of precise detail and uncertainty ('I don't know where – Southwold perhaps') gives an authentic feel to the narration. Remember this in your own writing. Memory can be a vital resource, as Glaister goes on to say:

Would-be writers often object that they have no memories to draw on, or that nothing interesting ever happened to them. This is not possible. Memory can be hard to access, but it's a skill that can be learned. And it's not so much interesting things but unique ways of seeing ordinary things [. . .] Catching one little tail end of a memory and patiently teasing it out can be a way to start. And it doesn't matter if the memory is not complete, nor entirely true. [. . .] A little kick start from the memory can set off your imagination – and who knows where that might lead . . .

(Glaister 2001: 78)

### *Raiding your past*

The more you write, the more you will raid your own past. These incursions won't diminish or reduce your memories – rather those recollections can be enriched and become more fully realised. As Jamaica Kincaid says of her writing:

One of the things I found when I began to write was that writing exactly what happened had a limited amount of power for me. To say exactly what happened was less than what I knew happened.

(quoted in Perry 1993: 129)

**17**

It's important to realise that you will not betray the truth of any particular memory by failing to stick steadfastly to certain details, or by not having a total recall of events.

There may be times when you will wish to use episodes or elements from your life experience more or less directly. Often you will use just fragments of your own past. You might like to use a single aspect of a character known to you, or a place, for instance. You might like to use a turn of phrase that your grandmother used; you might focus on the feelings of being lost on the first day at a new school. There is no rule for how much or how little you can use.

## Activity 1.6   Writing

Using the present tense, like Glaister does, write about a personal memory of either a place or a character in your notebook.

Make it brief, 250 words or so, but try to get as many sensory perceptions as possible going, and try to fix the memory in time, as Glaister does, so it is just one moment. Include everyday details and don't be afraid to admit one or two uncertainties.

### *Discussion*

This activity doesn't ask you to change anything from the way you remembered it, but you might have found yourself inventing things – some sensory perceptions, for instance. It is impossible to notice every little detail about an event or moment, let alone be able to recall such detail from the past. It is inevitable that you will invent even in this limited exercise. That invention should be welcomed, not resisted; it will always be guided by what you do know about the event.

### Conclusion: You know many things

'Writing what you know' is a large and rich project, one that provides an endless resource. The skill lies in reawakening your senses to the world around you, and then using what you find with discrimination. By realising the potentials of your own life experience, you will be collecting the materials necessary in order to write. 'Writing what you know' can amount to a lot more than you may have first bargained for. It doesn't mean that you are limited solely to your own life story, as the next chapter will illuminate further. Neither does it mean you have to be entirely true to your memories. Often a different kind of truth will emerge from the activity of writing about elements of your past and your everyday life. In this way, writing about what you know is a route to a different understanding of your own experience, and therefore also a route to finding out what you don't know.

## References

Glaister, Lesley (2001) in Julia Bell and Paul Magrs (eds) (2001) *The Creative Writing Coursebook*, London: Macmillan.

Heaney, Seamus (1980) 'Death of a Naturalist' in *Selected Poems 1965–1975*, London: Faber & Faber.

Lee, Laurie (1962) *Cider With Rosie*, London: Penguin.

# 2

# Writing what you come to know

*Derek Neale*

By using sensory perceptions and your own memories you are capitalising on your 'direct' experience of life. In this chapter you will do some more work with memory and using your imagination. You will look at the uses of research – or what might be called 'indirect' experience. We will step away from the literal gist of 'writing what you know', and look at the limitations of sticking too closely to such advice. If you only write about what is already known, then your writing might become tired and predictable. We will look at ways of reviving and reinvigorating it.

### Memory and association

In the last chapter you saw how memory can be viewed as a type of narrative. Of course, memory can be more than this – or less, depending on which way you look at it. Memory often works in a spontaneous manner, by way of association. You may catch a certain smell and all of a sudden you're cast back ten, fifteen or twenty years. You may feel a certain texture against your skin, hear a certain sound, and immediately think of another era. Pop songs offer an easy example of this. You may hear a certain song and be thrown back to your childhood, or to a time when, unlike now, the sun was shining and there wasn't a cloud in the sky, or to a time when you lived somewhere very different.

In Marcel Proust's *A la recherche du temps perdu* (*In Search of Lost*

*Time*) there is a famous moment where a chance combination of sensory perceptions rekindles a memory:

> One day in winter, on my return home, my mother, seeing that I was cold, offered me some tea, a thing I did not ordinarily take. I declined at first, and then, for no particular reason, changed my mind. She sent for one of those squat, plump little cakes called 'petites madeleines' ... No sooner had the warm liquid mixed with the crumbs touched my palate than a shiver ran through me and I stopped, intent upon the extraordinary thing that was happening to me.

> (Proust 2002: 51)

The 'extraordinary thing' provoked by the taste of the cakes and tea is the memory of Combray, a central place in the novel and the setting for a crucial part of the narrator's past. The passage highlights the ordinary nature of the events leading up to the flashback, and how the recall was totally dependent on chance. In this type of recall the past returns through mundane coincidences, often a chance perception – a smell, a song, a taste.

These chance associations occur frequently in real life and in literature. Look back over 'Death of a Naturalist' and the opening from *Cider with Rosie* in the last chapter. See how the writing operates around a group of memories and associations that in the end form a constellation of recollection, not just one single moment. Memory often works like this: one perception leads to a memory, which in turn leads to another memory and so on. These associative and resonant memories seem at first glance to be mostly unconscious, serendipitous and hard to predict. There are, however, ways of prompting such thought processes.

Now let's focus in more detail on associations and memories that are prompted by the senses.

### Activity 2.1 Writing

Use the sensory perceptions that you gathered in Activity 1.3 in the last chapter. For each perception write down an association from your own experience – a sentence for each at most.

Some of your perceptions might make you think of your childhood; they might remind you of something from yesterday or last week. Try to be specific. So, for instance, you might have listed the sound of a lorry driving past and it might make you think of the delivery driver who backed into the wall at the end of your street and how embarrassed he was. You might have listed the feel of the breeze through the window on your face and it might remind you of a different climate, a place you once lived perhaps, or a specific moment on holiday when the weather was especially good or bad.

### *Daydreaming*

You may have found that by seeking one association other associations followed; your mind might have started wandering. For instance, you might have started with the sound of a plane flying overhead and thought of a particular destination you once visited, pictured the airport perhaps, then thought of a place you would like to go, and then a place your neighbour went to recently, and then thought about the colour of their front door and how it clashes with their curtains, and so forth.

Some might consider this rambling way in which memory and thought processes work to be a form of 'drifting off'. Sigmund Freud suggested this is what the act of writing was all about. In his essay 'Creative Writers and Day-dreaming' Freud describes one possible model of how creative writing is related to childhood play, memory and fantasising:

A strong experience in the present awakens in the creative writer a memory of an earlier experience (usually belonging to his child-hood) from which there now proceeds a wish which finds its fulfil-ment in the creative work. The work itself exhibits elements of the recent provoking occasion as well as of the old memory.

(Freud 1964 [1959]: 139)

Notice how both the elements of past and present are used by the writer, according to Freud. In his opinion, the memory is usually connected to childhood, but this isn't always so. You aren't confined to a single part of your past; all of it can be used in your writing. Freud also notes how daydreams (and night dreams for that matter) can be boring and sometimes tiresome for those being forced to listen to them. The creative writer gets round this obstacle, according to Freud, by 'finding a suitable aesthetic form' – a story or poem – in which to express the daydream. In the preamble to finding that form (later chapters will help you to do that),

**23**

your notebook is the place to collect your perceptions and associations, where you have free rein to fantasise and wander (and wonder) aimlessly – or as Freud would have it, to daydream and to play.

## The limitations of 'writing what you know'

'Write what you know' is good advice on the whole and, as we have seen, it can mean a variety of things. However, if taken too literally and interpreted in too limited a fashion, such advice can be restrictive. If you know something too well, there might be no sense of discovery or revelation in the writing. It might lack energy. The key is to reinvigorate your memories, to shift certain elements from their original context, so those elements are seen afresh by you, and consequently by your reader. This will be explored further, later in this chapter. Now we will look at how thinking about the cultural context of specific memories might help your writing.

## Cultural memory

Our memories are an infinite resource, but are not just made up of personal moments and individual detail. We all exist within particular cultures and there are historical episodes that run parallel to our own lives. When John Major was prime minister, a student of mine wrote a short story with the following opening sentence:

> I guess, just as with the Major assassination in the late 20th century, everybody can remember exactly where he was and what he was doing on the day the space people brought Jesus back to Earth.
>
> (Greenaway 1994)

This dazzling start both embraces and imaginatively subverts shared cultural knowledge. John Major is referred to, but he is assassinated; Jesus is referred to, but he has been abducted by aliens. It also points to what has almost become a cliché – we knew where we were and what we were doing at certain historical moments: when JFK was killed; when Martin Luther King was assassinated; when Princess Diana died; when Bob Marley or John Lennon died; or on 9/11 when the twin towers were destroyed. Personal memories can often be associated with cultural memories and this shared knowledge can inform your writing. As well as historical events and characters, you can also use songs and films, and even television programmes.

### *Memory and nostalgia*

When using cultural memories in your writing, it's important not to use them just for purely nostalgic or conservative reasons. You can lose readers or not attract them in the first place if you are seen to be wallowing in your own past. Yet you should be aiming to capitalise on the warmth and energy of such memories. It's important to retain a focus and have a purpose when you use your past; beware of indulging your own nostalgia.

### **Activity 2.2   Writing**

- write down in your notebook some cultural details (songs, singers, films, historical events) from a period of your own past;
- list some personal details from the same period (like the names of roads and friends);
- pick a specific year and an event – it could be a cultural event like a pop concert, sporting event or television programme; it could be a more personal event like a school play, a homecoming, a wedding or a party.

Write either a poem (using no more than sixteen lines) or a piece of prose (up to 250 words) – which uses some of the cultural and personal details you've just gathered, and which focuses on the event you've chosen. The event can be a success or failure. For instance, you might write about the scoring of the winning goal in a cup final, or the school play in which you are humiliated by singing out of tune. Don't forget to use any pertinent sensory perceptions as well as cultural associations.

### *Discussion*

It is important that you make your memories dynamic and bring them alive rather than stick with staid perceptions. By changing key elements in your memory, you can sometimes learn more about what it is you are writing and what you want to write about. For instance, what would the episode that you recall look like through the eyes of someone else, someone who was also there perhaps?

Asking these sorts of questions about what you remember, then shifting the recall, can lend a new energy or perspective to your subject matter, reviving an over-rehearsed memory, so that you can discover it anew as you reveal it. This is a vital strategy, as you will now see.

## Imagination

Writers have always found ways to overcome the difficulties presented by subjects that are either too close to them or just beyond their direct experience. Their solutions fall into two camps: research, which we will touch on shortly, and the use of imagination.

'Use your imagination' is an imperative phrase that has come to be used in everyday conversation as a sort of mundane exhortation. It usually means something along the lines of 'think a bit harder'. In the context of the creative process, 'imagination' holds other connotations, many of them grander than this first assertion. It can suggest powers of invention, impersonation and also a semi-mystical process involving chance and inspiration whereby you wait for the bright idea to come along.

Although these connotations might be relevant sometimes, it's important to retain that first mundane definition, whether you're jotting something down in your notebook or preparing a final draft. Imagination *is* thinking harder. But remember, 'thinking harder' doesn't necessarily mean thinking in more difficult ways; it just means asking more questions. Imagination is a way of exploring possibilities, and going beyond what you immediately know. It is not necessarily mysterious, though it can undoubtedly be magical in terms of what it might produce. It isn't an exclusive skill possessed by a talented few. We all possess imaginative powers, but not all of us use them as fully as we might.

## Activity 2.3   Writing

Write down five facts about a person you know well. These facts can be just the straightforward details of their lives – their age, where they live, hair colour.

Now ask some 'What if . . .?' questions about these facts and write them down. So, for each fact come up with at least one alternative. You might have chosen a friend who lives next door but your new version will live in New York; your friend might be tall and now is short; might be a woman and now she is a man!

### *Discussion*

You might have found that asking one question is enough to launch a stream of further questions that need answering about how this new character might live in such a new location. Each and every life is surrounded by unfulfilled possibilities. By seeking out some of these possibilities you have started to use your imagination, and you have started to investigate the character in an intriguing way – by discovering what they are not. This is not just something to be done with people. You can also do it with places – what if the village wasn't actually in Yorkshire but in Devon? What if the café was in the main street and not in a back alley? What if it was a Balti curry house instead of greasy spoon? You can do it with sets of relationships too.

### Research

As a writer you will often have to gather other forms of knowledge in connection with your subject, the elements that lie outside your direct knowledge. This is something you will often need to do – research what you are writing about. Doing research means investigating and, to a certain extent inhabiting, the world you want to realise. Family memories and even direct knowledge aren't always enough to go on and you may need to supplement 'what you know'. Books will often be a vital source of information, but they aren't the only source. The internet will be a good source of further detail. Also, don't underestimate the value of field work. Sometimes you might like to take a trip to the local magistrate's court, to the Italian restaurant, to the pig farm or to sail on the ferry – to remind yourself of wherever you might be writing about.

### Activity 2.4   Research and Writing

Pick a brief item of news from your local newspaper or from the local radio or television news. Do some research about this item – using the internet, dictionaries or other reference books.

- Find out at least three further facts that you didn't previously know about the news article.
- Stick the original article in your notebook – or a summary of it, if it's a radio or television item.

- List underneath it or around it all the extra information you have managed to find.
- Write a fuller version of the item (in 200 words or less) including the information you have found.

For example, the news article might concern anglers catching fish in the local canal after a cleaning operation had countered pollution and years of neglect. The additional facts might include:

- the fish caught – carp – is bred for food in the Middle East (dictionary or encyclopaedia);
- where the canal runs to and from (local or national map);
- what the cargo carried on that particular canal used to be (internet or history book).

### *Discussion*

The type and depth of research you undertake will influence the course of your eventual writing. Sometimes research will not seem necessary, sometimes otherwise mundane events will be brought to life, made bigger, richer and more intriguing just by making a little effort and broadening 'what you know'. Sometimes this gathering of information will be included in your writing, sometimes it will be gathered and then discarded, having fulfilled its primary function – to convince you that you know what you are writing about.

### Conclusion: The creative process

Most psychological models of the creative process include an unconscious stage, sometimes called the 'incubation period', where ideas hatch and develop beyond our conscious control or awareness. The work you do in your notebook will enable you to make the most of this 'unconscious' potential. Part of the process is to let go, to allow the unconscious to come to the fore. Some writers engage in habitual behaviour while waiting for the hatching part of the process. Other writers profess to learn what they are writing about during the physical act of writing. There is no one formula for how it will work for you. You will have to find your own working practice.

The writing process has many aspects. As most of the models of creativity note, there is invariably hard work involved. You might persevere with an uncertain first draft, putting marks on the page for the first time. You might put in hours with the redrafting and editing. You might spend time mining your own past and present experience, and doing research to further your knowledge. You may come across ideas seemingly by accident or while asleep, or while occupied with something else entirely. To 'write what you know', or to write anything, is not a simple or straightforward matter. Yet it offers rich rewards. To finish a draft can be exhilarating. The feeling of simply writing in your notebook can be utterly absorbing, and sometimes rapturous.

It is important to remember that 'write what you know' is a liberating piece of advice, a route to discovery, not a limitation. Such advice invites you to explore what you know and therefore to understand it more fully. It reminds you to use every kind of knowledge at your disposal: conscious, unconscious, sensory, accidental, researched, imagined. It reminds you to seek and to scrutinise at all times, whether working in your notebook or on a final draft. You are the conduit carrying the words, the memories and biographies, from thin air into the world. You are the only carrier. It will always be this link to you, the writer, which will lend a piece of writing its vitality and aura of believability.

### References

Freud, Sigmund (1964 [1959]) 'Creative Writers and Day-dreaming' in *The Standard Edition of the Complete Psychological Works of Sigmund Freud*, Vol. 9, London: The Hogarth Press, pp. 131–41.

Greenaway, Quentin (1994) 'Jesus Christ or a Better Class of Zoo', manuscript (unpublished).

Proust, Marcel (2002) *A la recherche du temps perdu*, translated as *In Search of Lost Time*, Scott Moncrieff and Terence Kilmartin (tr.), revised by D.J. Enright, London: Vintage.

# 3

# Why write?

*Sara Haslam*

The first, and most obvious, answer to this question is: for pleasure. Reading books about people's lives is a hugely popular pastime – ask any librarian or bookseller. Writing them is part of the same fascination. In what follows we will explore both the pleasure and the fascination in more detail.

### Chapter I: I am Born

Whether I shall turn out to be the hero of my own life, or whether that station will be held by anybody else, these pages must show. To begin my life with the beginning of my life, I record that I was born (as I have been informed and believe) on a Friday, at twelve o'clock at night. It was remarked that the clock began to strike, and I began to cry, simultaneously.

(Dickens 1966 [1850]: 49)

The extract you've just read is the beginning of *David Copperfield*, a novel by Charles Dickens. It may be fiction, but it raises issues crucial to the exploration of life writing and how it works. One of those issues concerns fact versus fiction, because how can anyone prove what they have only been told? Another is to do with the function of memory: incomplete memory doesn't prevent Copperfield from writing about himself. Both these issues will feature to a significant degree throughout the rest of this book; here they also help to focus our attention on why life writing is such a compelling genre.

*David Copperfield* has been described as Dickens's 'veiled autobiography', so it is a form of life writing as well as a novel (Drabble 1989: 256). In its opening paragraph Dickens conjures with two of the most common reasons for writing autobiography, or biography, come to that. One is the desire to establish or record a series of truths, however that word is qualified. The other is the desire to tell a story about a developing – improving, changing, or simply growing up – self. It's a story which includes heroes, as Dickens says (and probably villains as well), to be recognised by the reader through his or her encounters with fiction. The emphasis on the word 'story' is important, though at first it might seem surprising in this context (remember that fiction and life writing developed in close proximity to one another in the 1700s). But in one sense all anybody is doing when engaging in life writing is giving a narrative shape – a curve, an arc, or even a loop – to a story of a life. 'I had long wanted to set down the story of my first twenty years', writes Simone de Beauvoir in the preface to her autobiography (de Beauvoir 1965 [1960]: 7). Though Dickens starts his story with birth, there are many other ways to begin. One biography of de Beauvoir opens when she's in her seventies, keeping vigil at the bedside of a dying Jean-Paul Sartre (Francis and Gontier 1992 [1987]: 1).

The desire to record events, and to tell a story, may be among the more common reasons people write in this genre, but there are others. What might some of them be?

## Activity 3.1   Writing

Consider the life writing you have read or know about, and why these books might have been written. If it would be helpful, you could search your shelves, or those in the biography/autobiography sections of a bookshop or library, for examples as you investigate this question – there is often a clue early in the text. Make a list in your notebook of some of the reasons you come up with.

### *Discussion*

My list of reasons is given below, and I've also included some texts to illustrate them. It's not an exhaustive list, so you may have come up with further reasons of your own.

People may write auto/biography:

- To experiment with a new perspective on a life, perhaps by bringing increased subjectivity or objectivity to bear. A biographer of actor/ director Orson Welles claims that during her research Welles spoke to her 'freely and openly as I dare say he has never done before'. She was able then to communicate how 'Orson himself felt about it all' (Leaming 1987 [1985]: vii).
- To compete with other narratives on the subject, correcting, developing, or rebutting information they contain. Quotations from the cover of a John Lennon biography provide good examples: '*Lennon* is acknowledged as the definitive portrait of the complex, charismatic genius' and includes 'rare illustrations', we are told (Coleman 1995 [1984]).
- To establish a particular narrative order over a life. Gore Vidal is concerned very much for the form of his autobiography, appropriately called *Palimpsest* (1996 [1995]). (A 'palimpsest' is a parchment that has been prepared for writing on more than once.) Vidal 'starts with life; makes a text; then a *re*-vision – literally, a second seeing, an afterthought, erasing some but not all of the original while writing something new over the first layer of text' (Vidal 1996 [1995]: 6). A revealed relationship between the past and the present is crucial to his approach.
- To look for answers to specific or more general questions, or to explore states of mind. 'Writing this book [. . .] clarified for me Sexton's distinctive achievements as an artist', says Diane Wood Middlebrook of her biography of the poet Anne Sexton (Middlebrook 1992 [1991]: xxi). Travel writer Bruce Chatwin demonstrates a similar approach in a journal: 'this book is written in answer to a need to explain my own restlessness – coupled with a morbid preoccupation with roots' (Chatwin 1993: 13).
- To get it off the chest, or to find some kind of peace. Writer Ford Madox Ford dedicated the first volume of his autobiography to his two daughters; he wanted to present to the next generation his knowledge of life (Ford 1911: vii). My own great-aunt, Ethel Cox, who was childless, felt a similar urge when about to undergo an operation aged 95. She dictated some autobiographical notes to my mother.
- To provide a personal witness statement, or testimony, to a cultural or

historical event. Anne Frank's writing, about which you will read more later in this book, is an example here.

- To make money, or to enhance celebrity. Model Jordan (Katie Price) begins her autobiography with a dramatic hook for potential readers, promising that 'I've held nothing back' (Price 2004: ix).

Of course, things may well be more complex than this implies. Jordan, or Vidal, or Leaming, may have had more than one reason for writing (setting the record straight *and* making money, for example). The creative impulse must have been involved – to varying degrees – too. But the reasons for writing seem pretty clear here nonetheless. In other examples of life writing they may be less apparent. We will explore this idea shortly.

Life writing authors often indicate some of their reasons for writing in the title that they choose, so this can be a valuable place to start looking for clues. The name of the subject will almost always appear (it would be interesting to try and find an example where this isn't the case), but there is often extra and valuable information present too.

### Activity 3.2  Reading

Compare the following titles. What might they be saying about why each book has been written?

1   Kate Chisolm, *Hungry Hell: What it's really like to be anorexic: A personal story*
2   Agatha Christie, *An Autobiography*
3   David Jenkins, *Richard Burton: A brother remembered: The biography Richard wanted*

#### *Discussion*

1   The title addresses the reader as an equal, or even a friend. Its hard-hitting red-top alliteration, and the extended subtitle with its conversational abbreviation make me feel as if I'm eavesdropping. Which in a way I am, because the title describes the telling of a 'personal story' in confessional form. It is carefully worded to avoid alienating any potential reader; it positions itself self-consciously 'on the level'. So the title indicates the desire to reach as

wide a readership as possible with a story designed both to make an impact and inform. The strong implication in the word 'really' is that readers will find awful details here about anorexia that may be missing from other similar narratives: Chisholm seems to want to attract even prurient attention. Here we have a multi-pronged, no-holds-barred attempt to sell the book, at a time when anorexia occupies a powerful place in the cultural milieu (it was published in 2002).

2 The second title is curious. The choice of the indefinite article stands out: why should it not be **The** *Autobiography*? Possibly Christie is leaving room for the writing of a later, different narrative. But it's more likely that she's signalling her understanding of the fact that, as she wrote, she was able to tell only one of many possible stories about herself. She had to make narrative choices – where to begin and where to end, for example. Her memory and how she used it will have affected these choices, as will other likely variables (like her word limit). Overall the tone established by her title is hesitant, provisory, and creative, as opposed to definite and factual. Christie uses it to show that she is writing to provide the reader with infor-mation, even as she warns that she's not aiming at a complete or definite picture in narrative. She is strikingly different in approach from our final author.

3 In this title David Jenkins lays biological claim to his subject by calling him his brother – a fact Richard's stage name disguises – thereby self-consciously setting his narrative apart from others about Burton. As he is related to his subject, presumably he wants to persuade potential readers of his superior ability to produce an authorita-tive narrative. While Christie cultivates a sense of plurality with her title, then, he communicates a belief in a hierarchy of narratives with his own version at the pinnacle. He also seems to take another swipe at unauthorised versions (those written without the consent or assistance of the subject), by referring in the title to the subject's desire for his text. One inference a reader could make is that Jenkins is also writing in order to correct some wrong: there's a high level of defensiveness in the length of the title.

Though it may seem hard at first to relate some of the discussion of these last examples to the pleasures of life writing, there are forms of satisfac-tion to be found there. Reflect on this broad exploration into the reasons others may have for attempting life writing, or return to the initial list you made, as we now consider why you might want to practise this craft.

## Activity 3.3   Writing

Write down in your notebook what some of your own reasons might be for creating a life writing narrative. Remember as you complete this activity that life writing can be shaped into poetry as well as into prose. A section of Alice Walker's poetry collection *Revolutionary Petunias* is devoted to autobiography (Walker 1988 [1973]: 1–25), for example. Remember also that creative processes are transformative: use of the first person in a poem does not necessarily mean it is exclusively autobiographical.

### *Discussion*

Whether you have one clear reason, or several, for your writing, do refer to them from time to time as you progress through this part of the book. Reminding yourself of your reasons for writing may well assist you in the choices you will make as you complete activities and plan your writing. If you can't quite formulate an answer to this question, remember that all writing is in part an act of discovery: your reasons may become apparent only as you progress. A more tentative, exploratory approach can work just as well. You will see in Chapter 8 how the biographer Richard Holmes sometimes follows unexpected subject matter, seeking to recover what he calls 'lost voices' in his narratives, the voices of those 'tiny moon satellites' around the gigantic famous figures of the past.

In our discussion so far we have been investigating some of the more evident reasons why people may choose to create life writing narratives. Something like fame, or competition, or simply a need to set things down (or even a combination of all three), spurs writers into action. But earlier I said that other reasons why people may write are less apparent, or less specific. Many life writing narratives seem generated, for example, by the experience, or perception, of loss. Perhaps this is something you listed when completing the first activity in this chapter.

You no doubt can recall texts in which loss is powerfully central. The loss that seems to drive the writer might be of a loved one, or of a place, like a home, perhaps. (So David Jenkins's narrative is relevant here too.) Stella Tillyard's biography of three eighteenth-century sisters, *Aristocrats*, opens forcefully, with destitute women queuing up to abandon their babies to the newly-formed Foundling Hospital in Hatton Garden, London, in 1741 (Tillyard 1995: 1–3). The loss can also often relate to a concept, to an ideal, or to a state of happiness, health or innocence. In the sub-genre of narratives written by people who know they are suffering from life-threatening illnesses, the writer is one who is both doing the losing and anticipating being lost. Examples of these narratives, often searingly painful to read, are Oscar Moore's *PWA* [or Person With Aids] (1996), John Diamond's *C: Because cowards get cancer too* (1998), and Ruth Picardie's *Before I Say Goodbye* (1998).

These perceived or experienced losses seem to sting the author into a written attempt to account for, or to moderate, them. Creativity can be a way of countering and answering difficulty or suffering. We will explore some examples of texts like this in Chapter 5.

### Into words

In the following activity you're encouraged to practise some of the ideas we have discussed so far, and the links between them.

### Activity 3.4   Writing

Imagine you have a biographical subject, X, who was born somewhere in the world in 1914. In your notebook write two paragraphs, of up to 150 words each, on the following:

- In the first, invent four more facts about him or her, and then try to educate your reader about your subject.
- In the second paragraph, imagine that your subject has been forced by circumstance to leave a much-loved house. Describe this circumstance, and its impact on your subject.

### *Discussion*

You're dealing with a fictitious character here, rather than an actual biographical subject, but, as you know, imagination and creativity always play a part in the construction of life writing narratives. In the discussion of Dickens's 'veiled autobiography' I drew your attention to the need to choose a place to start, for example, and the idea that readers look for stock characters from fiction as they read life writing. You will hear more about this in Chapter 8, and how Richard Holmes, for instance (as mentioned after the last activity), talks of his work running along the 'fault-line' between fact and fiction, implying that sometimes it's hard to separate one from the other.

For the second of your passages I gave you the basis of a plot with which to conjure: a cause and effect scenario with likely and imaginable emotional as well as physical consequences. This brief outline meant that narrative considerations might have been to the fore as you wrote. The first paragraph demanded a more informative role, and you were working with a 'factual' framework which you may have enjoyed. But as indicated above the development of the story will be important in this example too. If you come back to this activity later in this book, think how you might improve this aspect of it. A good place to start will be to consider the relationships you want to make between your facts.

As a conclusion to this chapter, you're going to explore the role of imagination in autobiographical life writing. You will be writing about your birth, and when you do this you can't help but activate the relationship between fact and fiction (which you'll look at in detail later in this book). To political thriller writer John le Carré his birth is one his 'imagination insists' on (le Carré 2003: 22).

### Activity 3.5   Writing

Write a piece with the title 'Chapter 1, I am Born', or 'Poem 1, I am Born'. It can be either a 150 word prose piece or a 10–16 line poem.

When you have done this ask yourself the following questions about your paragraph or poem:

- Which elements are fiction/imagination, and which are fact?
- Does the paragraph/poem hint at your reasons for writing?
- What might make a reader want to read more?

### *Discussion*

Dickens used a combination of fact and fiction as he wrote his opening to *David Copperfield* – he was actually born on a Friday (Ackroyd 2002

[1990]: 1) – and this is a common approach to take. As none of us can remember the occasion consciously, we must decide either to investigate in some way our unconscious minds as we research our births, or choose to rely on information passed on by others. Time and memory can combine to make that information less accurate, and more like fiction, than we might like to think. Feelings or memories that emerge from the unconscious must be treated with similar caution. But a blend of these processes may well prove fruitful and effective when translated into life writing. The best-selling *Road to Nab End* opens with a good example: 'the fierce rattling of my bedroom window-pane first roused me from the long sleep of birth' (Woodruff 2002 [1993]: 9). In his poem 'The Fifth Philosopher's Song', Aldous Huxley sets the 'Me' he was born as against the 'million million' others he might have been instead (quoted in Allott 1962 [1950]: 125):

> **The Fifth Philosopher's Song**
> A million million spermatozoa,
> All of them alive:
> Out of their cataclysm but one poor Noah
> Dare hope to survive.
>
> And among that billion minus one
> Might have chanced to be
> Shakespeare, another Newton, a new Donne –
> But the One was Me.

The blend of fact and fiction in this poem acts as a way of questioning the roots of identity and ideas of self-worth.

Compelling birth stories, you may think, and they are. Nonetheless there is another way to deal with this time of our lives: we can choose to acknowledge the lacuna (or missing part) which is at the beginning of our memory. Crime-writer P.D. James does just this in her autobiography, in which she avoids any fictionalising of her own birth: 'I seldom have a birthday without thinking back to that date which none of us can remember, at least not consciously; the moment of birth' (James 2000 [1999]: 4). Her approach stands in stark contrast to that taken by Woodruff and Dickens. Here James admits to a general lack of memory, which all of us will recognise, but she also suffers from a more specific factual absence that may resonate with some readers too: 'I must at some time have been told the time of my birth, but I have forgotten it and, as those present are now dead, it is one of those facts I shall never know' (James 2000 [1999]: 4). Novelist and life writer Jenny Diski was in a similar position, and found it to be a stimulating one. 'I've got no family to ask questions of', she says (in the Open University interview transcribed in Chapter 7) and then, crucially, 'that was the point, it's a blank slate essentially'. Basic information, like the time, and even the date – although this will be extremely rare – of your birth, may have been out of your grasp too. If that was the case, what choices in your paragraph or poem resulted from this? Did you decide to reconstruct that information, or to acknowledge its lack?

Your reflection on matters like this may help to ensure that your reasons for embarking on life writing, and your ways of interesting the reader, can merge in your text. If you need to find out what you think about your lack of memory, or information about some aspects of your life, and are using your writing to do so, your reader may well be able to identify with this process. Similar issues can apply when you're writing biography. Indeed, one way of understanding (and, like Jenny Diski, coming to welcome) these lacks may be plain in our post-Freudian world. Freud's idea of secret lives within us, the unconscious world, is culturally dominant whether we agree with it or not. As we write about ourselves, or another, the gaps in our knowledge and understanding will remain, and can be highly effective too. Writer Jackie Kay will help us to think more about why in Chapter 6.

## References

Abrams, M. H. (1993 [1941]) *A Glossary of Literary Terms*, Orlando, FL: Harcourt Brace.

Ackroyd, Peter (2002 [1990]) *Dickens*, London: Vintage.

de Beauvoir, Simone (1965 [1960]) *The Prime of Life*, Harmondsworth: Penguin.

le Carré, John (2003) 'A sting in the tale', *Observer* magazine, 7 December, pp. 22–39.

Chatwin, Bruce (1993) *Photographs and Notebooks*, David King and Francis Wyndham (eds), London: Jonathan Cape.

Chisolm, Kate (2002) *Hungry Hell: What it's really like to be anorexic: A personal story*, London: Short Books.

Christie, Agatha (1993 [1977]) *An Autobiography*, London: HarperCollins.

Coleman, Ray (1995 [1984]) *Lennon: The definitive biography*, London: Pan Books.

Diamond, John (1998) *C: Because cowards get cancer too*, London: Vermilion.

Dickens, Charles (1966 [1850]) *David Copperfield*, Harmondsworth: Penguin.

Drabble, Margaret (ed.) (1989) *The Oxford Companion to English Literature*, Oxford: Oxford University Press.

Ford, Ford Madox (1911) *Ancient Lights and Certain New Reflections*, London: Chapman & Hall.

Francis, Claude and Gontier, Fernande (1992 [1987]) *Simone de Beauvoir*, London: Minerva.

Huxley, Aldous (1962 [1920]) 'Fifth Philosopher's Song' in Kenneth Allott (ed.), *The Penguin Book of Contemporary Verse*, Harmondsworth: Penguin.

James, P.D. (2000 [1999]) *Time to Be in Earnest: A fragment of autobiography*, London: Faber & Faber.

Jenkins, David with Rogers, Sue (1993) *Richard Burton: A brother remembered: The biography Richard wanted*, London: Random House.

Leaming, Barbara (1987 [1985]) *Orson Welles*, Harmondsworth: Penguin.

Middlebrook, Diane Wood (1992 [1991]) *Anne Sexton: A biography*, London: Virago.

Moore, Oscar (1996) *PWA*, London: Picador.

Picardie, Ruth (1998) *Before I Say Goodbye*, Harmondsworth: Penguin.

Price, Katie (2004) *Being Jordan: My autobiography*, London: John Blake.

Tillyard, Stella (1995) *Aristocrats: Caroline, Emily, Louisa and Sarah Lennox 1740–1832*, London: Vintage.

Vidal, Gore (1996 [1995]) *Palimpsest: A memoir*, London: Abacus.

Walker, Alice (1988 [1973]) *Revolutionary Petunias*, London: The Women's Press.

Woodruff, William (2002 [1993]) *The Road to Nab End*, London: Abacus.

# 4

# A preface

*Sara Haslam*

### Introduction

In this chapter you will work towards writing a statement about a life writing text that you want to attempt, in poetry or prose. It might be helpful to think about this statement – which you will create as the final activity in the chapter – as being like a preface, or foreword, which a writer uses to explain the 'subject, purpose, scope and method' of a book (*Oxford English Dictionary*). There will probably be more than one narrative in this genre, shaped in more than one way, that you would like to write, but the first section of this chapter should help you to narrow this down to one that you can work with for now. It will also introduce you to a range of prefaces and the jobs that they do.

### Prefaces

In Ruth Picardie's *Before I Say Goodbye* (1998), the preface is used by her husband to provide a brief biographical account of Picardie, as well as to explain how the rest of the book has been compiled (mainly from her columns in the *Observer Life* magazine, and emails to and from Picardie). The reader learns about Picardie's work as a successful journalist, and the breast cancer that ended her life prematurely, and is thus supported in the encounter with her own words. Max Arthur's *Forgotten Voices of the Great War* is a very different kind of life writing narrative. It's a collection of autobiographical sketches by men and women who fought on the Western Front and in Gallipoli during the First World War. He uses his preface to discuss the source of the material and the methods he has used to edit and to arrange it; he also makes links between the kinds of narratives involved and, perhaps most interestingly, reflects on issues of accuracy and the 'truth' of memory (Arthur 2003 [2002]: preface). Having read his preface, a reader is poised to engage with his book, and may well find it more useful or informative.

I've already used a brief example from the preface of Middlebrook's biography of Anne Sexton in the discussion of why people write. In it Middlebrook explains her aims, and also discusses the sources of her material: she tells us that she is writing with the full co-operation of Sexton's family, and was invited to undertake the task by the poet's daughter (Middlebrook 1992 [1991]: xx–xxii). Her preface establishes her credentials, then, as well as setting out that, for example, she intended to honour some of Sexton's attitudes to life by writing her book. Alice Walker's preface to *Revolutionary Petunias* is also thought-provoking. It reveals that the poems are 'about Revolutionaries and Lovers; and about the loss of compassion, trust, and the ability to expand in love that marks the end of hopeful strategy [. . .]'. Walker continues, 'They are also about (and for) those few embattled souls who remain painfully committed to beauty and to love [. . .]' (Walker 1988 [1973]). While there are significant differences between these four examples of life writing, in style, content, and form, their prefaces perform a similar function: they prepare a reader for what is to come. This is what your preface should aim to do.

## Your preface

The first decision to make before formulating your own statement is whether you intend to experiment with autobiographical or biographical writing. We're going to explore this choice. In each of the sections that follow I raise key issues which should stimulate your thinking, and help you to write your preface. Marge Piercy's pithy statement of the differences between biography and autobiography provides a productive starting point. She writes that 'autobiographers know everything; biographers never know enough' (Piercy and Wood 2002 [2001]: 89). Your work in the last chapter – on memory and on birth, for example – means that you know that this statement requires substantial qualification, but its provocative nature might be useful too.

### *Autobiography*

Though I consider this form in detail in the next chapter, I want to introduce you to two ways of categorising prose autobiography. Think about which of the following categories you would like to find yourself in:

(a) writers who relish their subjectivity (the 'me-ness' of the narrative);
(b) writers who in the main use the autobiographical frame to comment on the world at large.

### Activity 4.1  Reading

Read the following extracts from *Portrait of a Marriage* by Vita Sackville-West and *A Passage to Africa* by George Alagiah. Consider which illustrates a more objective and which a more subjective narrative position.

### from *Portrait of a Marriage*

Of course I have no right whatsoever to write down the truth about my life, involving as it naturally does the lives of so many other people, but I do so urged by a necessity of truth-telling, because there is no living soul who knows the complete truth; here, may be one who knows a section; and there, one who knows another section: but to the whole picture not one is initiated. Having written it down I shall be able to trust no one to read it; there is only one person in whom I have such utter confidence that I would give every line of this confession into his hands, knowing that after wading through this morass – for it is a morass, my life, a bog, a swamp, a deceitful country, with one bright patch in the middle, the patch that is unalterably his – I know that after wading through it all he would emerge holding his estimate of me steadfast [. . .].

I start writing, having spent no consideration upon this task. Shall I ever complete it? and under what circumstances?, begun as it is, in the margin between a wood and ripe cornfield, with the faint shadows of grasses and ears of corn falling across my page.

(Sackville-West 1992 [1973]: 9–10)

## from *A Passage to Africa*

> In the aftermath of September 11, people were fond of saying that
> the 'world had changed'; that life would never be the same again.
> What they meant, of course, was that life in the rich world, and
> especially in America, had changed. In the poor world nothing
> much had changed at all, except that many more countries would
> be regarded with suspicion and many more of their citizens seen as
> potential terrorists. Very quickly, Somalia found itself on the list of
> those nations deemed to pose a threat to America's security. This is
> the country that the USA backed in the Cold War and then tried to
> save from famine in 1992.
>
> [. . .]
>
> *A Passage to Africa* has been a few months in the writing but
> literally a lifetime in the making. While the events it covers reflect
> the preoccupations of a conventional, Western newsroom – where
> I have worked since early 1989 – my response to what I have
> witnessed is coloured by a much earlier experience. As a child,
> Africa was my home: my family moved from Ceylon, as it was
> then, to Ghana when I was six.
>
> [. . .]
>
> [This book] is, primarily, about Africa, but it is also about how I
> came to think about Africa in the way I do.
>
> (Alagiah (2002 [2001]: 4–5)

### *Discussion*

It's probably fairly clear that I have chosen the Sackville-West extract as
an illustration of a subjective narrative style. The Alagiah extract, though
evidently still autobiographical, displays a dedication to wider subjects
too. Contemporary politics and recent world history are foregrounded by
Alagiah; they do not feature in Sackville-West's writing. The back cover
of Alagiah's text makes this disparity more clear; it describes the book as
'an autobiography not so much of George Alagiah, but of Africa itself'.
Sackville-West's prose is, in contrast, dedicated to a self-reflexive journey
through 'my life'. Other perspectives only intrude when they justify the
need for the narrative; the 'I' is remorselessly repeated, circumscribing
the world she wants to reveal. Although the Sackville-West extract is the
shorter of the two, forms of 'I' ('I', 'me', 'my') occur more frequently, as

you may have noticed. (One way of thinking about this difference in form is that Sackville-West's 'I' seems from this extract at least to be comparatively geographically settled.)

Hillary Rodham Clinton's autobiography illustrates a further form of subjectivity – one that seems to combine these two approaches. Though the reader is very aware of the 'I' (look how many times it's used), her subjects are American history, politics and culture as well:

> I wasn't born a first lady or a senator. I wasn't born a lawyer or an advocate for women's rights and human rights. I wasn't born a wife and mother. I was born an American in the middle of the twentieth century, a fortunate time and place. I was free to make choices unavailable to past generations of women [. . .]. I came of age on the crest of tumultuous social change and took part in the political battles fought over the meaning of America and its role in the world.
>
> (Rodham Clinton 2004 [2003]: 1)

Subjective it may be, then, but her *Living History* is about momentous and widely-relevant events too.

One textbook on creative writing suggests that autobiography, and I would guess especially the more subjective kind, can only be profitably indulged in when the writer is famous: 'successful autobiographies are usually written by people who have done something of outstanding significance' (Burton 2003 [1983]: 173). I don't agree with this way of determining success. Life writing bookshelves often display auto-biographies by people whose names are otherwise unknown, but which sell well. J.A. Cuddon writes that 'since the Second World War almost anyone who has achieved distinction in life – and many who have not – has written an account of his life' (Cuddon 1992: 73).

I tend to agree with the approach Marge Piercy and Ira Wood take to this issue. They talk about the way it is helpful, when writing auto-biography, to universalise individual experience, or render it in a more objective form – especially if fame isn't involved! Even if you do look inward, looking outward and finding ways of making your narrative engage your readers is necessary too (Piercy and Wood 2002 [2001]: 220, 89). And Nigel Nicolson, editor of the Sackville-West text (as well as being her son), provides an example of how one might go about this.

'*Portrait of a Marriage* is a story of how love triumphed over infatuation', he writes in the introduction to the 1992 edition. Calling it a story offers his, and more importantly his mother's, readers one way of identifying with the text, making its subjectivity resonate more widely; this idea takes us back to our early thinking about *David Copperfield*. Offering a recognisable, universalising theme like love provides another way; as a theme it may well encourage readers to form a relationship with Sackville-West's text.

One final thought in this respect concerns the sub-genre of travel writing. Books like Bruce Chatwin's *In Patagonia* (1979 [1977]) are written in the first person, charting as they do individual experience, but they can be about a good deal else besides. Chatwin explored a part of the world that was seldom visited, and through observed or researched incident and anecdote he evoked its distinct character for his readers (from the adventures of Butch Cassidy to drilling for oil in Tierra del Fuego). *In Patagonia* offers a universalising theme in its representation of a largely unknown place, as well as, perhaps, in what it has to say about wandering and exile. If you have travelled, and are interested in experimenting with less obviously subjective autobiography, travel writing may be the form for you. The freedom granted by the lack of settled perspective could well be attractive too.

### Activity 4.2   Writing

What might you offer a reader by way of a universalising theme in an autobiographical text? Write down some of your ideas in your notebook, and remember to come back to them as you write your statement if you decide to opt for an autobiographical narrative.

### *Discussion*

There is simply no right answer here, as you may imagine. Each life is different. *In Patagonia*'s offerings in this respect were discussed briefly above. In Pete Hamill's autobiography, *A Drinking Life* (1994), it is the contemporary New York culture of drink that offers a universalising theme. The back cover proclaims that 'Hamill learned early that drinking was an essential part of being a man, inseparable from the rituals of celebration, mourning, friendship, romance, and religion'. Further examples I can think of from autobiographies include:

- living and fighting through a war;
- experiences of migration, adoption and disability;
- dependency on drugs;
- losing a parent at a young age;
- employment in a particular field like education or health, which many people in the world encounter at some point in their lives.

More generally, most life writing narratives explore the sense of time and history moving on – issues associated with ethnicity or sexuality may be particularly relevant here. Focused exploration of one of these issues, perhaps in a way that ranges more widely than your own individual experience, would provide you with a way of stimulating recognition, and interest, in those reading your work. As a final suggestion in this respect, the act of memory itself can be a compelling and universalising component of autobiography. All autobiographies depend upon memory, though to varying degrees.

### Biography

Biography too can depend on memory, of course, if you choose to write a narrative based on someone known to you. Whether you do or whether you don't, there are related formal decisions to be made here too.

### Activity 4.3   Reading

Read the extracts from *Paula* by Isabel Allende and *Funny Peculiar* by Mark Lewisohn. As you read them, consider the effect that is created by the emotional distance, or lack of it, between the writer and her or his subject. Which effect would you be more interested in emulating if you were to write a biographical narrative?

### from *Paula*

**Epilogue**
In December 1991 my daughter, Paula, fell gravely ill and soon thereafter fell into a coma. These pages were written during the interminable hours spent in the corridors of a Madrid hospital and the hotel room where I lived for several months [. . .].

> Listen, Paula: I am going to tell you a story, so that when you wake up you will not feel so lost. The legend of our family begins at the end of the last century, when a robust Basque sailor disembarked on the coast of Chile with his mother's reliquary strung around his neck and his head swimming with plans for greatness.
>
> (Allende 1996 [1995])

## from *Funny Peculiar*

> Summon up an image of Benny Hill and chances are it will be of a moony, schoolboyish face with comfy-cushion cheeks, piercing, naughty blue eyes and a mischievous smile, leering at an underdressed 'Hill's Angel' and speaking in a country-bumpkin's voice.
>
> This is the man who became the world's most popular comedian in the television era. And indeed Benny Hill was a great comedian. His strength lay in comedy architecture, characterisation, mime, delightfully light vulgarity and a facility to redeploy jokes of all vintages.
>
> (Lewisohn 2003 [2002]: Preface)

## *Discussion*

These narratives could hardly sound more different. The Allende extract is highly personal and emotionally charged, dealing as it does with the death of her daughter, encouraging the reader through empathy to situate him- or herself in the narrative. The other was also occasioned by a death but is, instead, distantly laudatory, light and conversational as it looks back at a figure many people in Europe would recognise by sight (and beyond – apparently Benny Hill is also big in Japan and the US). Both narratives may draw in their reader, therefore, but in the former this would probably be by way of a personally driven empathetic response. In the latter, Hill's television career, and the buoyant prose which describes it, establishes a greater sense of distance between reader and Lewisohn's subject even as he or she begins to read.

In the next activity we're going to explore these different approaches as life writers.

### Activity 4.4   Writing

Choose one person from your own life, and one public figure. Identify an aspect of both lives you would like to research – a favourite pastime, perhaps, a characteristic behaviour pattern, or a typical day at work. Find out three or four relevant facts in each case and write them up into two paragraphs of up to 150 words each, or two poems (10–16 lines). This is an exercise in which you're simply practising some biographical skills, so don't go into too much detail. Research may include talking to friends or family, and using your bookshelves, or those in a bookshop or library, or the internet.

Reflect on the process once you have completed the writing, and produce a third paragraph of 250 words in which you assess your paragraphs or poems, and how you produced them. Questions you might explore in it include: did you find one flowed more easily than the other? Why? Does your writing sound as though you identify more closely with one subject than the other? Is this effect something you wanted to achieve?

### *Discussion*

In completing this activity you've explored two kinds of biographical writing, and the links between them. Research is necessary whatever form of biography you choose, though this will be undertaken in different ways. The last part of the activity encouraged you to think about your relationship with your subject, and how it might be made explicit in a piece of biographical writing. The results may have been surprising here – perhaps you feel there was a high level of imaginative identification with the public figure, for example? You may want to adapt this final paragraph when it comes to writing your preface in the last Activity of this chapter.

### *The facts of the matter*

Although you will consider fact versus fiction in more detail in Chapter 6, and in the subsequent chapters too, you need to be able to say something about it in your preface. You may be most aware of dealing with facts as a life writer, or you may not; what follows should help you to explore and to test this awareness. Richard Holmes' image of the 'fault-line' between fact and fiction will be a useful one to hold in mind as you work through this section.

Perhaps you think you may brazenly adopt Ford Madox Ford's attitude to fact in his memoir of Joseph Conrad. He calls his text a 'novel' and a 'work of art', then writes 'it contains no documentation at all; for it no dates have been looked up; even all the quotations but two have been left unverified, coming from the writer's memory' (Ford 1989 [1924]: preface). Ford wanted to preserve his sense of how things were, his impression of events, which for him represented important kinds of truth. He could not be challenged by his subject, who died before he wrote his biography, but Orson Welles's biographer recounts the potentially awkward appearance of 'inscrutable disparities between what Orson remembers and the data' she unearths (Leaming 1987 [1985]: 2). Surprisingly, this does not prove to be a hindrance: Welles revels in this part of the process of being written about, though is adamant that the truth of the matter remains unresolved (Leaming 1987 [1985]: 3).

Such productively imaginative relationships with facts as those described above are truly engaging but are also, perhaps, rare. Ford's career in general suffered due to a reputation for a cavalier attitude to fact, and Welles is unusual in the strength of his positive, interested feelings towards being 'biographised'. Indeed, Welles applauds the consciousness-raising element of the whole process: 'one has organized one's life [. . .], and forgotten – perhaps deliberately and certainly unconsciously – what one wants to forget, and here is somebody coming up with the proof of things you're forced to remember or believe happened. I see the situation as a fascinating way to get into what a man's life is really like' (Leaming 1987 [1985]: 3).

Others may not display such an open, generous attitude to new or disputed 'facts'. My guess is you would have to choose the subject of your life writing narrative carefully to find one prepared, as Welles says he was, to be told things are not as they seemed. Bear in mind that there is a moral issue here too: what if something you discover may cause your subject or someone they know pain? True, to avoid this possibility you could make that subject yourself, and write autobiography. But active thinking and research can dislodge forgotten or buried memories and experiences in the autobiographer: you also would have to be prepared for them to come.

### *The status of your text*

The first issue for your consideration here is whether the text you are writing may be one you could aim to publish, or whether it is something you are writing for yourself alone. Even if you already know that you are writing for yourself, the statement you are currently engaged in developing will prove an important part of your preparatory work. If you think you may have different plans for your text, further questions for your consideration under this heading include:

- Will it be the only title on this subject, or one among many and therefore engaged in competition?
- If the latter, how might it make its mark?
- If the former, how might it appeal to a wide readership?

These issues can be explored using published books.

### Activity 4.5   Reading

On a recent visit to my local bookshop, I counted seven different biographies of Diana, Princess of Wales. Below I describe the back covers and blurbs of two of these biographies. How is each used by the author and publisher to advertise the status of their text? (NB: This relates to the discussion of motives in the first activity in Chapter 3 and you might like to look back to that to help you.)

(a) *Diana: Story of a princess*, by Tim Clayton and Phil Craig (2001). The back cover describes the book as 'the acclaimed international bestseller, revised and updated, telling the full story of the quest for the truth about the life and death of Princess Diana'. Further quotations on the back cover include one from the *New Statesman* ('intelligent and well-researched . . .') and the *Observer* ('good, plain, lucid, responsible').

(b) *Diana: In pursuit of love*, by Andrew Morton (2004). The back cover is a collage formed of photographs of audio tapes, and notes and letters to and from Diana. A publisher's note at the beginning of the text verifies the photographs (they are of the actual artefacts), and describes them as evidence of Morton's close relationship with his subject.

## *Discussion*

Both texts take their place as one among many books about Diana. The Clayton and Craig cover seeks to make its mark by stressing its learnedness and, perhaps, objectivity (although it can't resist the lure of the 'full story'). The Morton cover, on the other hand, goes unashamedly for the personal touch, with photographs of Diana's handwriting and tapes of her voice suggesting the mark it is making belongs to the subject herself.

Having practised negotiating some of the key issues associated with this genre in preparation for writing your own preface, we're now going to read one (nearly complete) biographical version.

### Activity 4.6   Reading

Read the preface to Dennis Overbye's biography (though note his qualification of the term) of Albert Einstein. Make notes on its treatment of issues related to its genre, its use of fact, and its status as a text. If you need to, refer back to the discussion of these issues in this and the previous chapter.

### from Einstein in Love

As of this writing Albert Einstein has been dead for forty-five years, but in his absence he seems more present than ever. He remains the scientist most likely to make front-page newspaper headlines, as modern science confirms yet another of his bizarre-sounding hypotheses, published long ago. Within the last two years, astronomers have discovered that a strange repulsive force, known as the cosmological constant, which Einstein dreamed up in desperation while trying to explain why gravity didn't cause the universe to collapse in on itself, seems to be shoving the galaxies further and further apart. The hottest thing in physics labs these days is Einstein-Bose condensate, an exotic new form of matter whose existence Einstein first predicted in 1932; the substance itself was first created only in 1995. Even Einstein's brain, preserved for four decades, made news in the summer of 1999, when neuroscientists at Macmaster University in Ontario announced that his parietal lobe, a region associated with math and spatial relationships was 15 percent larger than a normal person's. Time magazine capped the millennium by naming Einstein its Man of the Century.

From a distance, the trajectory of Einstein's life looks mythic. The one-time humble patent clerk, with his corona of white hair and the haunted eyes, who overturned the universe and gave us the formula for God's fire, who was chased by war and Promethean guilt to wander sockless like a holy fool through the streets of Princeton, making oracular pronouncements about God and nature, has become an icon not just of science but of humanity in the face of the unknown. His visage, peering beneficiently out at us from coffee mugs, posters, calendars, and T-shirts, is familiar in every corner of the world. Behind the iconic face, however, was a human being, one capable—as all human beings are—of behaving in distinctly un-iconic ways.

I first made the acquaintance of this lesser-known Einstein in 1990, in New Orleans, during a meeting of the American Association for the Advancement of Science. The AAAS meeting annually draws a few thousand scientists to debate and discuss issues ranging from better ways to explore Mars to the ethics of the Human Genome Project. At the time, in one of the stranger episodes in recent Einstein scholarship, a small clique of revisionist historians was advancing the notion that Einstein had cheated Mileva, who became his first wife, out of her proper share of credit for the theory of relativity. One slow afternoon at the meeting, I stumbled into a heated debate on this subject and was mesmerized. It wasn't that I necessarily thought the assertion was true, but it seemed amazing to me that such a debate was even occurring, as Einstein had died in 1955; he was arguably the most famous man in the world, the very author of our modernity. In my naiveté about history, I'd always presumed the key questions about Einstein—how he invented his theories, the nature of his relations with lovers and loved ones—had long since been answered.

In fact, I had never been particularly interested in Einstein the man. Like everyone else, I grew up with the image of the cosmic saint, whose only peer was God. It was hard to imagine that he had ever been young. But as I sat in the auditorium in New Orleans that afternoon it came as a curious relief to me—and I suspect to some of Einstein's modern colleagues, who've had to labor in the shadow of his enormity—to hear young Albert described as a philanderer, a draft dodger, a flirt, a lover, a hustler, an artist, an errant son, an egregious poet, and a scuffling physicist, whose girlfriend was a feminist and a mathematician. Before my eyes, in a kind of miracle of time-reversal, Einstein shed fifty years. *So the old boy had some juice in him after all*, I thought.

The claim that Mileva had a part in the authorship of relativity came largely from a selective reading of passages in letters, recently published for the first time, that Albert had written to her during their student years. In their correspondence, he had talked about the scientific issues that relativity would ultimately resolve, as well as about details of their courtship, Albert's fights with his mother, and, most spectacularly, the birth of the couple's illegitimate daughter, Lieserl in 1902. (Mileva's half of the correspondence for the most part seems not to have survived.) When I began to look further into the alleged controversy over relativity's authorship, I found that the letters, fifty-one in all, were only the most sensational part of an avalanche of newly uncovered material about Einstein, material that had the potential to transform our whole understanding of the man, his life, and his science. [. . .]

Strictly speaking, this is not a biography of Einstein—there is already an abundance of those on the bookstore shelves. Instead, my goal has been to bring the youthful Einstein to life, to illuminate the young man who performed the deeds for which the old man, the icon, is revered. Over the last seven years I've gone through five eyeglass prescriptions, reading hundreds upon hundreds of published and unpublished letters, squinting with my research assistant, Val Tekavec, at Einstein's cramped handwriting. I've followed him as he discusses everything from the details of space-time metrics to how his children should brush their teeth. I've tracked down every place Albert and Mileva lived, separately or together, and have walked the streets of their neighborhoods, eaten cheap wurst in student-quarter cafes, as they must have done. I've read Einstein's high school transcripts and his divorce papers. I've clambered on the razor-edged Säntis Mountain where Einstein almost lost his life as a teenager, walked in the Engadine Alps where he and Marie Curie took a famous hike in 1913, and snaked up perilous switch-backs retracing Albert and Mileva's trip up to Lake Como and over Splügen Pass (where their lost daughter, Lieserl, was conceived in 1901). I've sought out descriptions of Einstein and his friends, in order to plague them with embarrassing questions about their ancestor's behaviour.

No history, especially a narrative one, can escape the charge that it is, on some level, a fiction, an inexact blending of a writer's subjective choices, interests, and prejudices with the data of the documentary record. While the Albert Einstein portrayed in this book is of necessity partly my own creation, thoughts or feelings that I attribute to Albert or Mileva are drawn from letters or other of their writings. When I speculate about what someone's thought processes might have been, I've taken pains to clearly signal in the text that I'm out there alone on the thin ice of history.

Doubtless there will be among the readers of this book physicists who are uncomfortable with the detailed treatment of Einstein's romantic and family affairs, while there will be many nonscientific readers put off by discussions of Einstein's physics. But no exposition of Einstein could pretend to completion if it did not explore both the sacred and the profane aspects of his existence.

(Overbye 2003: x–xiii)

### *Discussion*

Overbye makes a clear case for how his biography will make its mark, despite taking for its subject an enormously well-known and much written about man. The initial section of his preface covers familiar territory, detailing all the ways in which Einstein's fame and importance is demonstrated in the world. But then he goes on to explain that by focusing on the young Einstein, he, Overbye, has found original, untrodden ground. His book may then appeal to those who already know a great deal about the scientist, but will also provide non-specialists in the field with a gentle introduction to physics and to a great thinker via human and universalising concerns. Overbye may also be pitching his narrative towards a particular kind of reader or scholar: those who are interested in gender politics, and look to restore to women their rightful place in cultural and intellectual history. Finally, Overbye also has something to say about the interaction between fact and fiction in his text. He recognises the role his own interests have had in determining the direction of his narrative, and acknowledges that it is, in some ways, 'a fiction'; but he also vouches for the extent of his research into original documents – research that is incorporated into his depiction of his characters and key foundational events in their lives.

Overbye's text provides a good example of how you can say something new about a famous subject. Remember, though, that you can also choose to write about someone known to you if you're going to opt for biography. The relationship between fact and fiction, research, and how your text will make its mark are issues for equal consideration should autobiography be your choice.

## Activity 4.7   Writing

If you have not already done so, pick the subject for your preface. You also need to decide whether you are planning a text in poetry or prose. You will want to cover the issues set out throughout this chapter whoever your subject is, and whatever your chosen form may be. Read back over the sections 'Autobiography', 'Biography', 'The facts of the matter', and 'The status of your text', if necessary. It might also be useful to go back to the definition of a preface at the start of this chapter, and to reflect again on Piercy's statement too ('autobiographers know everything; biographers never know enough').

Write your prefatory statement, of about 750 words, in which you set out your reasoning for the choices you have made regarding the treatment of your subject, including use of fact, textual status and other issues related to biography/autobiography. Don't worry at this stage about publication; simply think of this exercise as describing what you are setting out to do with your life writing narrative.

### *Discussion*

You will return to this subject in the next chapter and you may decide that this narrative is one you would like to spend more time developing. If time permits, it may also be worth experimenting with the preface process again. Perhaps you might like to try writing a preface for a different subject – biographical if you went for autobiography in this activity, or for some travel writing, for example?

## References

Alagiah, George (2002 [2001]) *A Passage to Africa*, London: Time Warner Books.

Allende, Isabel (1996 [1995]) *Paula*, Margaret Sayers Peden (tr.), London: Flamingo.

Arthur, Max (2003 [2002]) *Forgotten Voices of the Great War*, London: Random House.

Burton, Ian (2003 [1983]) *Teach Yourself Creative Writing*, London: Hodder Headline.

Chatwin, Bruce (1979 [1977]) *In Patagonia*, London: Pan Books.

Clayton, Tim and Craig, Phil (2001) *Diana: Story of a princess*, London: Hodder & Stoughton.

Cuddon, J.A. (1992) *The Penguin Dictionary of Literary Terms and Literary Theory*, London: Penguin.

Ford, Ford Madox (1989 [1924]) *Joseph Conrad: A personal remembrance*, New York: Ecco Press.

Hamill, Pete (1994) *A Drinking Life: A memoir*, New York: Little, Brown & Co.

Leaming, Barbara (1987 [1985]) *Orson Welles*, Harmondsworth: Penguin.

Lewisohn, Mark (2003 [2002]) *Funny, Peculiar: The true story of Benny Hill*, London: Pan Books.

Middlebrook, Diane Wood (1992 [1991]) *Anne Sexton: A biography*, London: Virago.

Morton, Andrew (2004) *Diana: In pursuit of love*, London: Michael O'Mara Books.

Overbye, Dennis (2003) *Einstein in Love: A scientific romance*, London: Bloomsbury.

Picardie, Ruth (1998) *Before I Say Goodbye*, Harmondsworth: Penguin.

Piercy, Marge, and Wood, Ira (2002 [2001]) *So You Want to Write: How to master the craft of writing fiction and personal narrative*, London: Piatkus.

Rodham Clinton, Hillary (2004 [2003]) *Living History: Memoirs*, London: Headline.

Sackville-West, Vita (1992 [1973]) *Portrait of a Marriage*, Nigel Nicolson (ed.), London: Orion.

Walker, Alice (1988 [1973]) *Revolutionary Petunias and Other Poems*, London: The Women's Press.

# 5

# Finding a form; writing a narrative

*Sara Haslam*

## Introduction

In this chapter, we are going to think more about the form (or, perhaps, forms) you might use in a life writing narrative. 'Form' simply means the organising principles of writing, as opposed to its substance or content. In this chapter, then, I discuss the various formal choices you will make as you construct your narrative, and offer examples from published texts. The activities encourage you to engage with and to practise a range of autobiographical and biographical forms.

## Activity 5.1    Reading

In this introductory activity we're thinking about the effects of formal choices. What strikes you about the form of the quotation below?

> I wake up in the night and there's a big dark shape leaning over me [. . .]. We live in a room in another woman's house, Mammy, Daddy and me and the baby. We are going out somewhere and my daddy is squatting on his hunkers in front of me tying my laces. He's swaying back and forth and this way and that and there's a queer smell about his breath and all at once he staggers back cursing, still on his hunkers, and nearly falls into the fire.
>
> (Boyle 2002 [2001]: 13–14)

### Discussion

I found the use of the present tense to be particularly striking as I read this passage from near the beginning of John Boyle's *Galloway Street: Growing up Irish in exile*. It creates a strong sense of immediacy, and also makes it easier for a reader to identify with the scene that is being described. Also of note is the way in which the passage combines the perception and language of a child (it's a somehow cocooned perception and the voice uses matter of fact sentences to describe what could be much more frightening and shocking; a child can't identify the smell as that of alcohol) and those of an adult (for whom, in the retelling, it's clear that the scene had an impact). It is a rich combination; time itself seems to become fluid in the way that his adult mind and memory give him some information, yet also withhold some from the child's persona which, for now at least, is narrating. Choices like this, about form, play a crucial part in the ways in which your narrative will take shape. Early consideration of the structural elements that underpin any piece of writing means greater freedom later on.

As further introduction to our in-depth work on form, I want briefly to offer a new way of dividing life writing into types. In the work you have done so far, you have mainly considered genre headings like 'biography' and 'autobiography' (sub-genres like 'diaries' and 'travel writing' have featured too and will do so more strongly in the remaining chapters of the book). But there are also categories of narrative method that it will be useful for you to address as you think about how you might like to write.

The first method is more fragmentary. In this category you might include autobiographical poetry, diaries, journals, letters, photographic records, and also narratives like John le Carré's memoir 'A sting in the tale', discussed below, or Jean Rhys's *Smile Please* (1981 [1979]). In *Smile Please*, an autobiographical text, Rhys simply collects a series of vignettes. Short chapters, for example 'Poetry', 'My Father', or 'St Lucia', grant Rhys a structure which means she doesn't have to provide a coherent, linking narrative. Horror writer Stephen King adopts a similar approach, stating matter-of-factly at the beginning of his book *On Writing: A memoir of the craft*, 'Don't bother to read between the lines, and don't look for a through-line. There are *no* lines – only snapshots, most out of focus' (King 2001 [2000]: 4). There is a sense of liberation for King in the lack of 'through-line'; and his visually suggestive word, 'snapshots', for what he provides instead may apply to aspects of Rhys's technique too. King's snapshots are short, numbered chapters that are often simply a page in length and relate, for example, a scene or memory to which he adds brief comment.

The second narrative method you might describe as being more continuous or connected. Here the more traditional kind of biography and autobiography might be found, in which prose links up sections of memories, and the appearance of a coherent and in some ways complete narrative is attained. Mary Benson's biography of Nelson Mandela reads more like a narrative without gaps, or with the gaps filled in, unlike the examples of Rhys and King:

> Nelson Rolihlahla Mandela spent his childhood in a fertile valley among the rolling hills of the Transkei. The family *kraal* of whitewashed huts was not far from the Mbashe River which flowed past maize fields and a wattle plantation, past grasslands where cattle grazed and on eastwards to the Indian Ocean.
>
> In that setting Mandela's love for his country and for his people took root. He was born on 18 July 1918 at Qunu near Umtata, the capital village of the Transkei 'reserve'. As one of the royal family of the Thembu, his upbringing was traditional and a sense of responsibility was bred in him.
>
> (Benson 1986: 15)

Although some life writing narratives may sound more complete than others, there is need for caution here. The nineteenth-century novelist Anthony Trollope mused on the practice of writing autobiography in his own attempt. He suggests that producing a complete narrative – telling everything – is 'impossible'. 'Who could endure to own the doing of a mean thing?' he asks, let alone write absolutely everything down (Trollope 1992 [1883]: 1). Trollope is right to ask these questions, and a complete narrative would be impossibly unwieldy, but a different answer to the moral question he raises had already been provided a hundred years earlier by Rousseau in his *Confessions*. Towards the beginning of his text, Rousseau writes that 'I have displayed myself as I was, as vile and despicable when my behaviour was such' (Rousseau 1953 [1781]: 17). Rousseau aimed to include shameful acts, hence the title of his autobiography (though he does not, in fact, present himself as completely 'vile'). His life writing narrative might then be said to be more complete in key respects than Trollope's version.

In the rest of the chapter you may find it useful to bear these methods – the more fragmented and the more connected – in mind, as a way of both helping you to make formal choices, and to make further links between some of the sub-genres that are discussed throughout the rest of the book.

## Activity 5.2  Writing

Write about three separate incidents, memories or moments in your life or in someone else's. Each piece should be up to 50 words. Then try to identify a way of linking the three incidents, a 'through-line'. Did you relish the snapshot feel of the disconnected incidents, or did finding a through-line give you a stronger sense of narrative satisfaction?

### *Discussion*

My attempt at this exercise is given below.

> When I was 8 years old, I had a good friend at school called Sasha. A new girl, Stacey, joined our class and befriended me and Sasha. Gradually, Sasha and Stacey became better friends than I was with either of them. I lost touch with them both when I changed schools.
>
> We are planning our summer holiday this year. Brochures for holiday villas in France and Italy are collecting in the newspaper rack. But as we discuss it over a period of weeks we realise our thoughts are turning more and more to the cottage we often go to in Snowdonia, in the mountains, a place we love.
>
> I have been baking, as it is my daughter Maisie's first birthday tomorrow. We have planned games and invited some friends over for tea. A present we ordered for her was delivered this morning, and cards and gifts have been arriving for the past couple of days.

My through-line for these stories is the house in Snowdonia, and the place of friendship that it represents. When I was a child I often wanted to take Sasha there, as proof of friendship, though she never came. It is a place to which I have since invited many friends, and I was married in the valley. I want Maisie to take friends there as she grows.

Each of your three short paragraphs could be used as the basis for, or even to form, separate sections of a more fragmented narrative of the kind we discussed above. In fragmented form the paragraphs have immediacy; they might be described as life writing snapshots of an ordinary working mind on an ordinary day, or days. The mind, after all, moves backwards, forwards, and around and about, not in precise narrative order as it processes experiences and events. There is something refreshing about this method and its effects for me. But a through-line also offers satisfactions. It turns the paragraphs into the beginnings of a plot with which to conjure. It suggests a way of connecting the separate memories which means they can be investigated in more depth.

### Forms of autobiography

In this section we'll consider the characteristics of various forms of auto-biography and how you might employ them in a life writing text. I'm going to discuss, in turn, memoir, travel writing, diary, journal, and letters. Which might you like to write? Remember your version can be a combination of forms, and of narrative methods too. Ruth Picardie's autobiography includes journalism, emails, and letters to and from the author. Susanna Kaysen's *Girl, Interrupted* (2000 [1995]), also an auto-biography, incorporates photocopies of hospital admission forms, psy-chiatrist's reports, and case notes as well as more continuous reflective prose.

### *Memoir*

The word memoir comes from the French for memory (la mémoire). As you might expect, writers of memoirs often foreground the act of memory in the record they are producing; a memoir therefore can sometimes be structured in a fragmentary, snapshot, fashion. John le Carré's memoir focuses on his relationship with his father, and although (sounding a bit like the start of *David Copperfield*) it does begin with the subtitle 'On being born and other adventures' it is revealingly and effectively structured as a series of key events or discoveries, not a 'begin at the beginning' narrative. Entertaining examples include 'In which I am talent-spotted for the monastic life and chastised by an Austrian night porter', and 'a Great Ambassador and a Grand Hotel Deprive Ronnie of his Golf Clubs' (le Carré 2003: 36, 32). Between these key moments, there is little attempt to join the dots. The sense that is created is one of a life of episodes, without seamless transitions; the silence between episodes is intriguing, and, in some ways, accurately representative – who could, or would want to, write everything down?

Memoirs can also be written biographically – although they're usually fairly autobiographical biography – and the same kinds of characteristics may well apply. The extracts in the next activity, from John Bayley's memoir of his wife, Iris Murdoch, treat the memory of two swims in the Cherwell river outside Oxford. One takes place before they were married, and the other occurs many married years later, when Iris is suffering from Alzheimer's disease. In between, Bayley's narrative meanders through an account of some aspects of their life together, but it in no way has, or attempts, the feel of a 'complete' record.

## Activity 5.3   Reading

Read the two extracts from John Bayley's memoir of his wife Iris Murdoch. Describe their tone, and style, and the comparative impact they have on you. How successful do you find Bayley's opening as a narrative technique?

A hot day. Stagnant, humid. By normal English standards really hot, insufferably hot. Not that England has standards about such things any more. Global warming no doubt. But it's a commonplace about growing old that there seem to be no standards any more. The Dog Days. With everything gone to the dogs.

Cheerless thoughts to be having on a pleasure jaunt, or what used to be one. For years now we've usually managed a treat for ourselves on really hot days, at home in the summer. We take the car along the bypass road from Oxford, for a mile or two, and twist abruptly off on to the verge – quite a tricky feat with fast moving traffic just behind. Sometimes there are hoots and shouts from passing cars who have had to brake at speed, but by that time we have jolted to a stop on the tussocky grass, locked the car, and crept through a gap in the hedge.

I remember the first time we did it, nearly forty-five years ago. We were on bicycles then, and there was little traffic on the unimproved road. Nor did we know where the river was exactly: we just thought it must be somewhere there. And with the ardour of comparative youth we wormed our way through the rank grass and sedge until we almost fell into it, or at least a branch of it. Crouching in the shelter of the reeds we tore our clothes off and slipped in like water-rats. A kingfisher flashed past our noses as we lay soundlessly in the dark sluggish current. A moment after we had crawled out and were drying ourselves on Iris's waist-slip a big pleasure boat chugged past within a few feet of the bank. The steersman, wearing a white cap, gazed intently ahead. Tobacco smoke mingled with the watery smell at the roots of the tall reeds.
[. . .]
We trailed slowly over the long field towards the river. The heat seemed worse than ever, although the sun, overcast, did not beat down as fiercely as it had done earlier in the day. The hay had been carried away some time before, and the brownish surface of the field was baked hard and covered incongruously with molehills. The earth in them was like grey powder, and I wondered how the moles ever managed to find any sustenance as they tunnelled within it. A pair of crows flapped lazily away as we approached the river bank. Crows are said to live a long time, and I wondered idly if they were the same birds we had seen there on our bathing visits for many years past.

I wished we had managed to come earlier, before the hay was cut, and when wild flowers – scabious, white archangel, oxeye daisies – stretched over the whole field among the grass. It was not a lush river field, probably because a bed of gravel lay just below the surface. There were big gravel ponds not far away, by the main road, but this field was a protected area, a plant and bird sanctuary of some kind. Not a fish sanctuary however: there were sometimes a few fishermen about, who kept themselves to themselves and remained almost invisible among the reeds.

Our own little nook was seldom occupied however, and it was empty as usual today. Once we would have got our clothes off as soon as possible and slid silently into the water, as we had done on that first occasion. Now I had quite a struggle getting Iris's clothes off: I had managed to put her bathing dress on at home, before we started. Her instinct nowadays seems to be to take her clothes off as little as possible. Even in this horribly hot weather it is hard to persuade her to remove trousers and jersey before getting into bed.

(Bayley 1998: 11, 33)

## *Discussion*

Bayley opens his narrative in the time of the later swim, to which he returns in Chapter 2. In the later time, both at the start and in the second extract, it is the heat that he emphasises, a stagnant, oppressive heat which is successfully communicated initially by stark, short (breathless) sentences, and later by a slow drawn-out prose, which seems itself to be suffering under an oppressive force. By comparison, what stands out from his telling of their first swim is the swimming itself, their shared endeavour and excitement, and their nakedness. The sheer pace denoted in the monosyllabic 'tore our clothes off' and in the following sentence about the kingfisher struck me as the only times Bayley's prose gathers any speed at all. Later, Iris's costume signifies instead their increased distance from each other and from the sensuous pleasure the swim and nature used to afford. In the later time, too, Bayley is more alone: he struggles with her clothes; it is 'hard to persuade her'; she does not answer him and the sense of a shared jaunt really has gone. Although natural images provide continuity between the two periods (the water-rat and kingfisher, the moles and crows) it is significant that the flashing kingfisher is the emblem of forty-five years before, the flapping crow is that of the present.

I find this a successful technique, and its success is to do with the way in which it uses to full effect both the continuities and changes discernible in most lives. In fact it uses continuities to highlight the changes. Iris and John visit the same place, to do the same thing, but the experience is immeasurably different because of the physical, emotional and psychological changes wrought by the intervening years upon them both. The placed memories, separated in time but not by space, show more starkly than any more gradualist approach could do how much has changed. Transcendent, the river acts as a kind of through-line, joining times and experiences together so that they can be expertly and effectively compared. And so Bayley makes formal choices that are very different from King's, and although his memoir does not read like a complete record, it is far less fragmented than King's collection of snapshots. Life writers often make similar formal choices to Bayley: 'Through-lines' is the title of the penultimate section in this chapter, and these choices are investigated there.

### *Travel writing*

Travel writers use examples of both the more connected and the more fragmented narrative methods that we have been exploring. (And note that they also write biographically too.)

### **Activity 5.4   Reading**

Read the following extract, which begins at the end of Chapter 49 and continues with the opening of Chapter 50 of Bruce Chatwin's *In Patagonia*. Which narrative method seems most in evidence in this extract?

> The origin of the 'dog-heads' is to be found in the 'vizzards' or battle masks, such as worn by Genghis Khan's cavalry or the Tehuelches when they attacked John Davis at Puerto Deseado. Shakespeare could have picked them out of Hakluyt. But either way Caliban has a good claim to Patagonian ancestry.
>
> **50**
> In the British Club at Río Gallegos there was chipped cream paint and not a word of English spoken. The twin black smoke-stacks of the Swift Corporation's old freezer reared above the prison yard.
>
> (Chatwin 1979 [1977]: 94)

### *Discussion*

Chatwin's chapters are, in general, short: often a page or two, sometimes only a paragraph (and are like King's in this respect). What is made clear in the above extract is the way in which the chapters can also dramatically switch subject and, as a result, tone. It is part of the appeal of Chatwin's text that his wide-ranging narrative means you are never sure what may be coming next.

While travel writing narratives do tend to share the wide range of Chatwin's text – often delving into history, human geography and the nature of travel itself, for example – some adopt a more focused approach. Colin Thubron's *In Siberia* (1999) has only nine chapters, as against Chatwin's ninety-seven. Thubron's are given titles which vary from the poetic ('Hauntings') to the specific ('To the Arctic'), but each covers a particular remit in some detail, though it may also make detours. Such a structure could be of use to the travel writer aiming to create a narrative which 'joins the dots'.

## Diary

A diary is a record of daily events. It tends to be less detailed than a journal, which can also be defined in a similar fashion (though in the US, the word 'journal' means 'diary'). In respect of this sub-genre, and the two which follow, journal and letters, I would qualify the remarks I made earlier about acts of distinction not necessarily being required for publishing success in the genre of autobiography. Diaries, journals and letters, because of their intensely personal nature, are most often of interest to a wider reading public if they concern the life of someone who has made a name for him or herself in the public sphere, unless they emanate from an early historical period. Not everyone could expect to generate interest in the exclamation '5 December [1913]. How furious I am with my mother! I need only begin to talk to her and I am irritated, almost scream' (Kafka 1992 (1910–23): 244), or the observation 'Sunday 14 February [1915]. Rain again today. I cleaned silver, which is an easy & profitable thing to do' (Woolf 1979 [1977]: 34).

In these sub-genres there is perhaps less place, too, for the universalising themes that can resonate in a general reader, as we explored in the last chapter. If you decide to adopt one of these forms for a life writing narrative, I would suggest that you're also deciding not to aim at publication – unless, of course, you have performed that act of distinction likely to result in publishers' interest. Despite all this, novelist Susan Hill makes a clear case for what she thinks is demanded from a published diary, and she, in fact, does not mention the fame of its writer. She also suggests that universalising themes *can* find a place in this genre: 'If an insight into the human condition, wit, wisdom and a share in another's life and times are what most of us ask of a diary, the blessed ability to sketch a scene or sum up a person in a few perfectly chosen words must still come top. The best diaries are rich and yet succinct' (Hill 2004: 37).

### Activity 5.5    Reading

Find the diary of someone who interests you, either on your bookshelf, in a library or bookshop, or on the internet. Judge the level of daily detail that they include in their narrative, and ascertain whether the book was published during their lifetime – the preface or introduction will give some clues here, as will the date of publication. Do you think your interest in them is fuelled or lessened by the things you learned about them from their diary?

### *Discussion*

The level of detail to which you have been treated will depend partly on where and when the book was published – as well as on who the subject is, of course. How you view this information will be a matter of personal choice: some will be bored, offended or shocked by certain kinds of behaviour, others will be captivated by the same material. In respect of this sub-genre, it is worth considering whether the personal things you learned merely helped to fill in the background to the image of the person that you already have, or whether they would have been enough to generate a dedication to the writer if you had not heard of them. If the latter is true, the minutiae of everyday life could well in themselves hold some level of fascination for you, and you should bear this in mind as you approach your own life writing.

I asked you to consider whether the diary had been published during the writer's lifetime or posthumously because writing with intent to publish – less common in diaries perhaps, with some notable exceptions, like those by former Prime Ministers – may alter the voice in which the diary is written, and lead to fewer personal events being recorded. The traditional view of the diary as something hidden from all eyes except those of the writer is, however, changing. Privacy is not what it was. In Hill's article Alan Clark's diaries provide an example of those written to be published (Hill 2004: 36).

### Journal

A journal, as I indicated above, shares some important characteristics with a diary. It tends to focus on everyday events and experiences (and is etymologically related to the French word for 'day') as recorded by an individual subject. Journals can be associated with an anecdotal style, rather than the intimate tone or content that may be expected from a diary. (In other words, a journal may concentrate on striking events or thoughts.) In addition, a journal may provide substantial details about a specific project, perhaps, upon which the author is engaged. A journal can be a kind of workbook or notebook, like the one you have been using as you have worked through this book. Writers often keep journals – useful critical tools showing the development of their work. Novelist Katherine Mansfield records in hers in 1916 that she wants in a new work to 'make our undiscovered country [New Zealand] leap into the eyes of the Old World. It must be mysterious, as though floating. It must take the breath' (quoted in Alpers 1980: 189).

### Letters

This category is self-explanatory. Once more, published collections of letters are generally by men and women who are known to the public in some way. Though it may be tempting to place letters in a class of their own as they're written for a recipient, it is important to note that many diarists think of their text as a recipient (the 'dear diary' format). And as we know authors may write diaries or journals anticipating publication at a later date – and, therefore, a reading public. Theorists too might well make the point that when anything is committed to paper, an editor is at work, and thus the sense of a watchful, reading eye that is in some way separate from the writer's own is present. So, letters too can be viewed as a form of autobiography. Malcolm Bradbury published *Unsent Letters* in 1988. On the back cover he says he hopes the book 'will spare him the trouble of ever having to write an autobiography' (Bradbury 1988). In this collection he experiments with what he would have said to often imagined recipients, using the letter form as a targeted autobiography.

### Activity 5.6 Writing

Find an example of a diary, or journal, or a collection of letters, that you think fulfils some of Susan Hill's criteria ('an insight into the human condition, wit, wisdom, and a share in another's life and times [. . .], the blessed ability to sketch a scene or sum up a person in a few perfectly chosen words'). This could be the same diary that you used for the previous activity. Choose an extract, about a paragraph in length, and write about that paragraph and the way in which it fulfils these criteria.

#### Discussion

As you wrote about your paragraph I hope you had a sense of which aspect of its successes impressed you particularly. It may be this aspect that most obviously 'hooked' you as you were reading, and which you might like to think about emulating in a life writing narrative of your own. I've recently read the account of a bullfight in a letter from a young Ted Hughes to his parents. He was on a trip to Spain with Sylvia Plath and wasn't yet admitting they were married. This letter alone, written long before Hughes became famous (and published in a collection edited by Christopher Reid in 2007), is packed full of universalising themes, including ideas about sportsmanship, the nature of animals, drama, with some noteworthy gender politics too; it ticks all Susan Hill's boxes, and more besides.

### Other formal possibilities

Now that we've explored the main autobiographical forms, we're going to open our frame of reference. In this section we'll deal with life writing forms more generally, encountering further options for structuring both autobiography and biography.

'Bildungsroman' is a literary term taken directly from the German. It refers to a novel which charts the education and development of its hero or heroine as he or she comes to maturity. Famous examples include Goethe's *Die Leiden des jungen Werthers* [*The Sorrows of Young Werther*] (1774), Austen's *Emma* (1816), and Dickens's *David Copperfield* (1850). We have already noted the autobiographical nuances of Dickens's novel, and critics have discerned autobiographical qualities in other Bildungsromans, so it may not come as a surprise that the term can provide a useful, general way of thinking about, or planning, the structure of a life writing narrative. The Bildungsroman is particularly closely related to a sub-genre of life writing: the conversion narrative, or spiritual account. Good (though not contemporary) examples of this sub-genre, such as those by Anna Trapnel and Hannah Allen, may be found in Graham *et al.* (Graham *et al.* 1989: 71–86, 197–210).

Though Middlebrook's biography of Anne Sexton ends very differently from Copperfield's story (Copperfield muses in the penultimate chapter that 'my domestic joy was perfect, I had been married ten happy years' (Dickens 1966 [1850]: 939)), she uses some aspects of the Bildungsroman form. Section I describes how her subject becomes Anne Sexton through marriage, having been born Anne Harvey; Section II charts her transformation from 'Housewife into poet', and the milestones in her poetic development along the way; Section III, 'The prizewinner', culminates in a chapter called 'Money and fame'. The final section, 'The performer', deals with her suicide, but also the bestowal of her third honorary doctorate, her success with a play, and her appointment as a professor. Middlebrook provides an abbreviated sketch of her structure in the preface: 'during her eighteen years as a writer, Sexton earned most of the important awards available to American poets. She published eight books of poetry [. . .] and she saw her play *Mercy Street* produced off-Broadway. She was a shrewd businesswoman, and she became a successful teacher; though skimpily educated, she rose to the rank of professor at Boston University, teaching the craft of poetry' (Middlebrook 1992 [1991]: xix).

Pete Hamill's autobiography, *A Drinking Life* (1994), might be classed as adopting the Bildungsroman form. At the beginning of *A Drinking Life* Hamill is a young child, deeply affected by poverty, and by the absence and then the drinking of his father. He learns at first that 'even the weakest human being could take a drink and be magically transformed into someone smarter, bigger, braver' (Hamill 1994: 19). Later, his concern is to stop drinking, and the final chapter begins with the words 'One January afternoon, after five sober years, I went for another walk in the snow' (Hamill 1994: 265). Placing the past alongside the present in this way (just as Bayley does in his memoir of Iris Murdoch) helps to show, through contrast, how far he has come in his moral development. Also emphasising this aspect of his narrative, a couple of lines later he writes, 'if I had not yet repaired some of the damage I'd inflicted on [the children] and others, I was trying, I was trying' (Hamill 1994: 265). In expressing this sentiment, and perhaps anticipating success, he looks to the future too, and so all three tenses are employed, helping his narrative to resonate with the added power of recognisable fictional structure and form.

It is a relief to a reader to find that things can progress, and develop in positive directions: a life, so often a messy and chaotic affair, can be tamed and shaped like a novel. I am not suggesting that things were not as Hamill has written them, but rather that he has made a powerful choice in his narrative form, one that makes his story more than personal, closer to archetypal in that he moves forward out of ignorance and misery and towards happiness and freedom.

### Activity 5.7 Reading and Writing

Read the following extract from Pete Hamill's *A Drinking Life*. Identify aspects of the Bildungsroman form in the narrative.

One day I ran into Brother Foppiano again. He was nastier now, because he had bloodied me and made me cry and run. *Your old man's an Irish drunk, your old man* ... I realized I was being watched by other kids, including my former friend Ronnie Zellins, and I knew that this time I couldn't run. So I piled into Brother, frantic, afraid, but determined not to cry, not to 'give up.' He hit me and hit me, but I held on to him, tripped him, fell upon him, hit him, then felt his hard wiry arms lock around my neck. I struggled. I jerked. But I couldn't get free.

So I whispered the word: *Shazam.*

Nothing happened. Brother Foppiano tightened his grip and I tightened mine on him.

We might be locked in that violent embrace to this day if Ronnie Zellins's beautiful mother hadn't come along and ordered us to stop [. . .].

One Sunday afternoon, a week after my second fight with Brother Foppiano, my father ordered me out of Gallagher's. His face was loose and bleary again, the way it had been the day I first saw him drunk. I imagined him leaving the saloon, helped by one of the men, staggering down the street to our house, and Brother Foppiano emerging from hiding to start his cruel chant. I asked him to come home. Maybe I whined. Maybe I was annoying. I know I was holding on to his coat. He jerked the coat out of my grip, looked down at me, and ordered me in a harsh voice to go home to my mother. Hurt and angry, I ran outside.

But I didn't go home. I went directly to Foppiano's candy store. I was desperate now, even willing to fight Brother again to be sure that he wouldn't see my father drunk. I could punch him. I could tease him. Or I could talk to him, argue with him, maybe even try to make friends with him. I just didn't want him to see my father being helped down the block. But Brother wasn't around, not behind the counter, not in the back room. His father sat there, reading a newspaper and smoking a cigarette. And with a sense of relief, I looked at the comic book racks near the door. I had read most of the new comics and was not interested in the books about funny animals or high school girls. Then I found the very first issue of Master Comics. I began to read the story of Captain Marvel, Jr., and was lifted out of Brooklyn.

Hey, Mister Foppiano said, ya gonna read or ya gonna buy?

I handed him a dime and rushed home, clutching my copy of Master Comics. Back at 435, I read this issue over and over, watching a crippled boy named Freddy Freeman hobble on his crutches. Suddenly he said *his* magic word — 'Captain Marvel,' the name of his hero — and was transformed into a lithe, strong hero in a sleek blue gold-trimmed costume. After my fight with Brother, I knew that 'Shazam' didn't work for me; it probably was just a lie. But maybe it could work for others. Maybe words, like potions, were also capable of magic. And I wished that my father had a secret word too. He would come home from Gallagher's and sit in the kitchen and whisper . . . *Captain Marvel*. A lightning bolt would split the sky and there he would be: two legs, young, whole, like the man in that old photograph, his eyes sharply focused. He would smile at me and reach over and hug me and off we would go together to play ball.

That never happened.

After two years in the first floor right, we moved again.

The new flat was only a few blocks away, but it was another descent, into a harder, poorer world.

Seventh Avenue was a wide avenue with trolley cars of the 67 line moving in both directions. The steel wheels of those sleek green-and-silver 'streamlined' cars ran on steel tracks, and we would hear their squealing clattering sounds through the night; some of us heard those trolleys for the rest of our lives. The power lines were hidden in steel poles that made a deep bonging sound when you hit them with bats or pipes; from the tops of these poles cables fed the lines that ran above the trolley tracks. Those poles and lines and the steel tracks gave the avenue the look of an artist's exercise in perspective, with diminishing lines flowing away into infinity, or its equal: Flatbush Avenue at one end of the avenue, Greenwood Cemetery at the other. In the mind of an eight-year-old, both were as far away as Madrid.

Our building was 378, a tenement rising four ominous stories above the street [. . .]. I felt like a stranger as we waited outside for the large men from Gallagher's to arrive in a truck with our furniture and our stuffed cardboard boxes. My mother said, You'll like it here. But I looked up and saw fire escapes climbing the brick face of the building, as if drawn with rulers, and a strange canopy hanging over the edge of the roof, and a flock of pigeons circling against the hard sky. I shivered in the cold, and my mother told me to wait in the hallway. But I was afraid to go through that door. I didn't think I would like it here at all. I wanted to go back to 471 Fourteenth Street, my real home.

> Do they have roaches here? I said.
> My mother laughed. I hope not, she said.
> I don't want to live here if they have roaches, I said.
> Well, she said without much hope, let's wait and see.
> (Hamill 1994: 23–5)

When you have thought about aspects of the Bildungsroman form in the Hamill extract, write a 150 word paragraph or a 10–16 line poem in which you focus your attention on an aspect of development in a character. The character you choose can be yourself.

### Discussion

Several things occurred to me in respect of the Bildungsroman form as I read this section of Hamill's book. The broken friendships, which may always be remade or replaced, seem crucial, as does the magical realism of a small boy's faith in his comic book hero father (despite the harsh intervention of the older narrator telling us that 'that never happened'). In the early stages, Hamill's character is shaped by violence and fantasy, then the opening of the new chapter illustrates how things are getting worse. It is as though he is taking a further step in the descent into a particular kind of hell. But the entrance 'into a harder, poorer world' simultaneously offers the possibility of an exit, a hope that at some stage the process will begin to be reversed. The extract ends with a mother's invocation to 'wait and see' and, although this is said 'without much hope', her phrase ushers in the future, and focuses the reader's attention on how things will develop.

This activity focuses your ideas on transformations and turning points. If this way of shaping your writing appealed to you when you came to the second part of the activity, you might use it to make further decisions about structure as your thoughts for your life writing develop. Rites of passage, for example, could play a prominent part in your narrative or poem(s).

## The past and the present

In *Watching the Tree* (2001 [2000]) Adeline Yen Mah uses childhood memories of her grandfather to begin a text which is part autobiography, part history of Eastern thought. But she soon makes clear that she didn't understand the full significance of her relationship with him, or the wisdom he imparted to her, until many decades later (Yen Mah 2001 [2000]: 2). The rest of her book is structured, highly effectively, as a way of achieving that understanding: remembered conversations with her grandfather and other family members are brought into the present so that she can explore and acknowledge their influence. Stories he told her are sourced in Chinese philosophical writings dating from 2000 years before. The book is also a kind of dialogue between the past child and the present adult self – as she comes to understand, and expound, Chinese wisdom and belief.

As I noted in the first example in this chapter, John Boyle's *Galloway Street: Growing up Irish in exile*, formal decisions related to use of past and present can have impressive consequences. Yen Mah usually employs the past tense – with the exception of recalled dialogue – as she reconstructs her memories. Boyle opts for the present tense as he seeks to turn the then into the now.

In the preface Boyle discusses his decision to use his boyhood self as narrator. It was not what he intended to do. 'For years', Boyle writes, 'I had been tinkering obsessively with reminiscences about my childhood in Scotland, as if some clue might lie there to my present confusion. It did not help, I began to understand, that these events were being recalled and enhanced by the middle-aged raconteur I had become. Now I felt the need to re-discover – truthfully, without embroidery – the boy I had been' (Boyle 2002 [2001]: 10).

In his planning, and perhaps even in early drafts, Boyle worked with what might be described as a dual narrator, his older self and the boyhood self both commenting on events and experiences. He abandoned this formal choice, though, in what he seems to consider the search for greater truth. Boyle was living in exile, away from Ireland, and, crucially, this meant that the boy he had been was not only from a different time and place, but spoke a different language too. The 'two distinct voices' Boyle refers to really were distinct. One, his adult voice, was for commercial voiceovers, probably in standard English and received pronunciation; he used the other to speak from the place he came from, to articulate an original self. This prior voice, once he had begun to listen to it, undermined and challenged Boyle's life at a distance, standing 'on the sidelines [. . .], watchful, reproachful' [. . .]: ' "Cummoan", he says, "ye know fine there wis mair tae it than that" ' (Boyle 2002 [2001]: 11). He decided, in the end, to use it to tell his story.

### Activity 5.8   Writing

Think of a specific and significant event in your own life, or in the life of a subject you have done some research on already. First of all write a 150 word paragraph about the event using the past tense. Then write about it again, also in 150 words, but use the present tense. Afterwards, consider which felt harder work, and which more suitable for the task.

### *Discussion*

This activity encourages you to experiment with the effects created by different tenses – effects you can replicate in your own narratives. A childhood voice, evoked in the present tense, can be highly effective, but Yen Mah and Boyle made different decisions, in the end, about whether the past or the present was most appropriate for their stories. A combination of the two can also work well.

In his autobiography, titled *Experience*, Martin Amis constructs a narrative that might be said to be like the one Boyle originally imagined. *Experience* is formally structured using a series of dualities, or parallels. As he takes his reader into his narrative, and explains his methodology (and his reasons for writing), Amis writes that 'My organisational principles [. . .] derive from an inner urgency, and from the novelist's addiction to seeing parallels and making connections' (Amis 2001 [2000]: 7). (This addiction may apply to writers more generally, as we have seen.) Conversations he has with his father, Kingsley Amis, are recounted throughout the text, as are comparable conversations he has with his own sons. Extracts from novels, by him and by his father, provide another layer of comparison. Letters home from university allow the student Amis a narrative voice, though it is often qualified by the adult writer. Times collide as parallels show how much, or how little, has changed. (An important through-line is provided by Amis's disastrous teeth: you'll have to read the book to see how!)

It's a growing, but densely patterned, self that is emphasised here, then; Amis the child meets and challenges Amis the student and Amis the adult. It might be tempting to see this as a form of Bildungsroman, and yet as a whole the narrative is more chaotic than that. 'My life', Amis states towards the end of his autobiography, 'is ridiculously shapeless. I know what makes a good narrative, and lives don't have much of that – pattern and balance, form, completeness, commensurateness' (Amis 2001 [2000]: 361). But some lives are written about as though they do have a shape, as we have seen, and in a way that *is* how he has addressed his own, bringing the past and the present into measured and productive encounters with one another. As we proceed we will consider one further formal characteristic of life writing, one that can help very much to enhance the sense of developmental pattern in a life.

## Through-lines

Although Stephen King made it clear that his readers should not expect to find through-lines in his prose, such continuities can prove very useful as a way of structuring a text, both for the author and for the reader. They make up a crucial part of the writer's formal armoury, and can be particularly valuable to a life writer, in whom a sense of the relevance of echoes and resonances is often particularly developed.

Back in Chapter 3, in the discussion of reasons for writing, I talked briefly about narratives that seem to owe their existence to the experience of some kind of loss. We're going to spend some time now thinking about loss as a through-line, and how it can be used to structure a narrative.

### Activity 5.9    Reading

Read the opening extracts by John Diamond, David Jenkins, and Gillian Slovo. What kinds of loss do they display, and what kind of impetus is that loss granting to the narrative as it begins (and, by implication, as it progresses)?

### From C: Because cowards get cancer too

In 20 years' time, if – touch wood, please God, all of that malarkey – I am still around, how will I feel about a bad back? I mean, a *really* bad back – the sort of ricked back I had a few years ago when I thought a kidney had burst and I couldn't move for a couple of days, and announced that things couldn't possibly get worse than this, and that this was the greatest medical indignity a man could suffer.

Or a cold – how will I feel about one of those colds when you can't breathe, or think, or write or imagine what it was like before the onset of the cold? Will I still feel about those everyday reasons for giving up as I did before 27 March 1997?

(Diamond 1998: 7)

### From Richard Burton: A brother remembered

The mountains have changed more than the village since we were children. Once bare of trees, a vast free playground for us, they are now thickly planted with conifers, gold Japanese spruce and Sitkas with sharp blue-green needles. Where we ran and chased one another, walkers and picnickers now dutifully observe the paths of the Forestry Commission.

(Jenkins 1993: 1)

### From Every Secret Thing: My family, my country

An hour before she died my mother went shopping. In the company of one of her closest friends, Moira Forjaz, she left the house where they'd given lunch to fifteen. They were due to go their separate ways later that afternoon and so they drove in convoy. It was 17 August 1982 and Maputo's faded elegance glistened in the bright winter sun.

[. . .]

There is a photograph of her taken on the day before she died. I have it on my London wall – she stares at my back as I sit by my computer. I turn to look at her. I see her carefree, smiling, confident, at home and I conjure her up, as she must have been in those last hours, her feet clicking against the cobbled pavement, her neatly turned ankle lifted up into the ageing Renault 16 that she had shipped from England.

Turning away I close my eyes and am assailed by a different image: my mother as she had once been in England. I see a stylish, handsome woman who had never lost her passion for expensive clothes but who was showing the strain of an enforced exile, a husband who was constantly on the move and three angry daughters.

(Slovo 1997: 1)

### Discussion

In two of the narratives, Diamond's and Jenkins's, we are offered different experiences of terrible loss that might be compared if we read them as representing symbolic ejections from paradise. In Diamond's case, the date he was diagnosed with cancer forms an impermeable membrane between the innocent rage with which he used to greet a bad back or cold, and the appalling and new experience of the extremes of which illness is capable. We might imagine that the tension between his loss of innocence and the fact of his experience will now drive the narrative, as Diamond charts his new territory, without being able to forget the old. Indeed, the old is changed too by the new, for with experience alone does he know it as the innocent time that it was, by comparison, always and only by comparison.

Jenkins's narrative also opens by opposing the time before to the time after. He conjures up the Wales of his youth as a giant open playground, in stark contrast to the modern, constricting, capitalist adventure now sited there. In this case, we might imagine that the loss of the freedom of youth will form a significant theme throughout, and that Jenkins's sense of the pleasure and importance of home will, in later years, be compromised by what it had become. Another form of loss is yet more fundamental to this biography: that of his brother Richard.

Slovo's narrative has as its impetus a more complex experience of loss. Slovo's violent loss of her mother is the primary driver of the narrative.

But loss features biographically here too. I am interested, in formal terms, by the images of her mother that feature on the first page of her text. One is a photograph of her mother, taken in Africa, showing her to be 'carefree, smiling, confident'. The other is a mental image of a 'handsome woman [. . .] who was showing the strain of an enforced exile' in London. Her mother was most herself, and most happy, in the more recent image – the photograph. This establishes a painful contrast. Ruth First was happiest when most in danger, when in Africa, rather than when in exile. Exile demanded too high a price for her, but being at home in Africa meant the risk of assassination, a risk that became reality in Mozambique in 1982. A pattern is constructed in the first page, then, that we might see developing throughout. We have two different representations of the same woman, which each evoke loss of self, of country, and of life, in powerful ways. Slovo's narrative pays attention to them both, as she in turn relates her own loss of her mother.

### Activity 5.10   Writing

Make notes about whether your own explorations in narrative so far are rooted in loss of some kind.

### *Discussion*

If your focus has been primarily on autobiographical narrative as you have thought and written so far, it is to be expected that you have been particularly attuned to memories, of childhood perhaps, or of another previous time in your life. Memory is, of course, in some ways inseparable from the concept or feeling of loss (while it can also be experienced as restorative). But equally, perhaps, if you have seen yourself as a biographer of a more objective kind, loss may not fit with your idea of the basis for your narratives: discovery, or reclamation, may seem more appropriate roots.

Before moving on from this section, I would like briefly to outline for you some further ideas that provide through-lines in life writing narratives. These may help to give you ideas for your own writing:

- the desert – in Somalian writer Waris Dirie's autobiography, *Desert Flower* (2001);

- Englishness, and the way it affects character – in Sebastian Faulks's *The Fatal Englishman* (1997 [1996]);
- love – in examples including Sackville-West's *Portrait of a Marriage*, as we have seen;
- houses in different countries – in Hilary Mantel's *Giving up the Ghost* (2003);
- ghosts – also in Mantel (2003);
- food – in Nigel Slater's *Toast: The story of a boy's hunger* (2003).

## Activity 5.11 Writing

Return to the preface you wrote for a life writing narrative at the end of Chapter 4. Choose one of the through-lines from this list I have just given you, or another that suits your chosen focus. Use the through-line to take this life writing a stage further. Write the first paragraph of the text (up to 150 words), or the first poem (10–16 lines), and then write some notes exploring how you will develop it using the through-line in some structural way.

When you go back to your preface you may find that your thoughts have already moved on. Don't worry about this. Use this activity as a way of expressing that development. If you still like what you see there, simply revisit the plans that you made and begin to bring the text to life with this initial paragraph of prose or poem.

### *Discussion*

Through-lines provide one way of establishing a formal structure for your life writing, and they are valuable in this respect. But you may also want to think of them as a unique aspect of your writer's imagination. As the previous list should have made clear, through-lines are diverse and wide-ranging. Even more common examples, like love, may prove to be an important way of your getting the most out of your particular creative energies and interests.

## Poetic life writing

You may well have attempted some poetic life writing in response to activities so far. At this point I'd like to give you some examples of this form of life writing, to encourage you to think about whether you might be interested in exploring it further.

### Activity 5.12    Reading

Read the poems below by Elaine Feinstein. In her introduction to the poems in the anthology from which they are taken, Feinstein says that 'first and foremost, I wanted poems that were genuinely trying to make sense of experience' (Couzyn 1985: 115). As you read, think about the experience she is making 'sense of', and the poetic techniques she is bringing to bear to do so.

**Calliope in the labour ward**
she who has no love for women
married and housekeeping

now the bird notes begin
in the blood in the June morning
look how these ladies are
as little squeamish as
men in a great war

have come into their bodies
as their brain dwindles to
the silver circle on
eyelids under sun
and time opens
pain in the shallows to wave up and over them

grunting in gas and air
they sail to a
darkness without self
where no will reaches

in that abandon less
than human
give birth
bleak as a goddess

**Song of Power**
For the baiting
children in my
son's school class who
say I am a witch:
black is the
mirror you give me

drawn inward at siege
sightless, mumbling:
criminal, to bear three
children like fruit
cannot be guarded
against enemies.

Should I have lived sterile?
The word returns me.
If any supernatural power
my strangeness earns me
I now invoke, for
all Gods are

anarchic even the Jews'
outside his own laws, with
his old name
confirms me, and I
call out for the
strange ones with wild hair

all the earth over to
make their own coherence
a fire their children
may learn to bear at last
and not burn in.


**Marriage**
Is there ever a new beginning when every
word has its ten years' weight, can there be
what you call conversation between us?

Relentless you are as you push me
to dance and I lurch away from you
weeping, and yet can we bear to lie
silent under the ice together like
fish in a long winter?

A letter now from York is a reminder of
windless Rievaulx, the hillside moving through
limestone arches, in the ear's liquid the
whir of dove notes: we were a fellowship of three
strangers walking in northern brightness, our
searches peaceful, in our silence the
resonance of stones only, any celibate
could look for such retreat, for me
it was a luxury to be insisted on
in the sight of those grass-overgrown dormitories

We have taken our shape from the
damage we do one another, gently as
bodies moving together at night, we amend
our gestures, softly we hold our places:
in the alien school morning in the
small stones of your eyes I know how
you want to be rid of us, you were
never a family man, your virtue is
lost, even alikeness deceived us
love, our spirits sprawl together
and both at last are distorted

and yet we go toward birthdays and other
marks not wryly not thriftily
waiting, for where shall we find it, a
joyous, a various world? in fury
we share, which keeps us, without
resignation: tender whenever we touch what
else we share this flesh we
bring together it hurts to
think of dying as we lie close

                    (Couzyn ed. 1985: 117–20)

## *Discussion*

As suggested by her introduction, Feinstein often uses poetry to reconstruct, to chart and to reflect on autobiographical episode or incident, although she does so in different voices (ranging from the gentle though not idealised fluidity of 'Calliope in the labour ward' to the explosive sharpness of 'Song of Power'). In the three poems you have read she engages with a range of experiences: childbirth, dealing with taunting children, the challenges of marriage and family. In a further poem in the same series, 'Dad', she treats the recent death of her father ('Every day I grieve/ for your great heart broken and you gone'). Most striking to me, in terms of her poetic technique, is the way in which her images give life to the more fundamental rites of human existence incorporated in this list (birth, growing up, marriage, death). Appropriately, these images are powerful, sometimes archetypal: the Muse (Calliope is the Muse of eloquence and epic poetry), the witch, the warrior. In 'Dad', his role as a gardener, a provider of food, features prominently. Such images resonate, so that her words may help to make sense of, and creatively connect with, experiences beyond her own.

You may find that this form of life writing attracts you more strongly than prose. If so, then a combination of your work up to now and later in this book will enable you to attempt a life writing narrative – perhaps via a sequence – in poetry. For a variety of verse forms and subject matter, you could also explore Ted Hughes' collection *Birthday Letters* (1998), or the poems of Emily Dickinson (1830–1886) (Dickinson, 1999). In the next chapter, poetic life writing features towards the end of a discussion between three prominent writers of biography and autobiography (Michael Holroyd, Jackie Kay and Blake Morrison) reproduced here.

## References

Alpers, Antony (1980) *The Life of Katherine Mansfield*, London: Jonathan Cape.

Amis, Martin (2001 [2000]) *Experience*, London: Vintage.

Austen, Jane (1966 [1816]) *Emma*, Harmondsworth: Penguin.

Bayley, John (1998) *Iris: A memoir of Iris Murdoch*, London: Duckworth.

Benson, Mary (1986) *Nelson Mandela*, Harmondsworth: Penguin.

Boyle, John (2002 [2001]) *Galloway Street: Growing up Irish in exile*, London: Black Swan.

Bradbury, Malcolm (1988) *Unsent Letters*, London: Arrow.

le Carré, John (2003) 'A sting in the tale', *Observer* magazine, 7 December, pp. 22–39.

Chatwin, Bruce (1979 [1977]) *In Patagonia*, London: Pan Books.

Couzyn, Jeni (ed.) (1985) *The Bloodaxe Book of Contemporary Women Poets*, Newcastle: Bloodaxe.

Diamond, John (1998) *C: Because cowards get cancer too*, London: Vermilion.

Dickens, Charles (1966 [1850]) *David Copperfield*, Harmondsworth: Penguin.

Dickinson, Emily (1999) *The Poems of Emily Dickinson*, Cambridge, MA: Harvard University Press.

Dirie, Waris (2001) *Desert Flower*, London: Virago.

Faulks, Sebastian (1997 [1996]) *The Fatal Englishman: Three short lives*, London: Vintage.

Goethe, Johann Wolfgang von (1989 [1774]) *The Sorrows of Young Werther*, Michael Hulse (tr.), Harmondsworth: Penguin.

Graham, Elspeth *et al.* (eds) (1989) *Her Own Life: Autobiographical writings by seventeenth-century Englishwomen*, London and New York: Routledge.

Hamill, Pete (1994) *A Drinking Life: A memoir*, New York: Little, Brown & Co.

Hill, Susan (2004) 'Private lives', *Guardian* Review, 10 January, pp. 36–7.

Hughes, Ted (1998) *Birthday Letters*, London: Faber & Faber.

Jenkins, David with Rogers, Sue (1993) *Richard Burton: A brother remembered: The biography Richard wanted*, London: Random House.

Kafka, Franz (1992 [1910–23]) *The Diaries of Franz Kafka 1910–23*, Max Brod (ed.), London: Mandarin Books.

Kaysen, Susanna (2000 [1995]) *Girl, Interrupted*, London: Virago.

King, Stephen (2001 [2000]) *On Writing: A Memoir of the Craft*, London: Hodder & Stoughton.

Mantel, Hilary (2003) *Giving Up the Ghost*, London: Fourth Estate.

Middlebrook, Diane Wood (1992 [1991]) *Anne Sexton: A biography*, London: Virago.

Rhys, Jean (1981 [1979]) *Smile Please: An unfinished autobiography* London: Penguin.

Rousseau, Jean-Jacques (1953 [1781]) *The Confessions*, J.M. Cohen (tr.), London: Penguin.

Slater, Nigel (2003) *Toast: The story of a boy's hunger*, London: Fourth Estate.

Slovo, Gillian (1997) *Every Secret Thing: My family, my country*, London: Little, Brown.

Thubron, Colin (1999) *In Siberia*, London: Chatto & Windus.

Trollope, Anthony (1992 [1883]) *An Autobiography*, Oxford: Oxford University Press.

Woolf, Virginia (1979 [1977]) *The Diary of Virginia Woolf*, Anne Olivier Bell (ed.), London: Penguin.

Yen Mah, Adeline (2001 [2000]) *Watching the Tree*, London: HarperCollins.

# 6

# Life writers in conversation

## *Sara Haslam*

At this point in the book we are going to take 'time out' to indulge in some critical reflection, while reading the edited transcript of an entertaining and enjoyable as well as useful discussion between three popular and prolific life writers. Robert Fraser, who has written biographical drama as well as prose, chaired the discussion and introduces Michael Holroyd, Jackie Kay and Blake Morrison at the start.

What follows, then, is a record of an open, intimate and honest process of self-assessment and discussion among the writers, who met and talked in London in 2005. We see into the heart of these artists, and learn from them about the value and the craft of life writing. Below I provide a list of the main issues that they raise, some of which you have already encountered in this book, and some of which you will meet again in later chapters. As you engage with these issues, reflect on the writing activities you have attempted so far, and perhaps try some of them again in the light of what Holroyd, Kay and Morrison divulge about their experiences of writing lives.

The issues raised are:

- the idea that 'autobiographers know everything, biographers never know enough', which you will recognise from your work in Chapter 4;
- biographical motivation;

- what happens when imaginary truths are challenged by writing an autobiography;
- privacy;
- fact vs fiction;
- the relationship between the life and the work;
- life writing and the broader context: the world;
- style/structure;
- past and present;
- finding a voice;
- poetic life writing;
- the appeal of life writing;
- loose threads.

Robert Fraser (RF): 'Life without theory' is how Benjamin Disraeli described biography. If he was right it seems a bit perverse to turn biography itself into a topic for debate. In practice, though, it's difficult to ply this trade whether as biographer or autobiographer, without considering one's position. Am I an intruder? Am I twitching at lace curtains? It's the truth I'm supposed to be telling, but whose truth is it anyway? Should I be here at all? Dr Johnson, that biographer of poets, once claimed that he could write the life of a broomstick; what one wonders, would the broom handle have written about Johnson. Brooms sweep round corners, they disturb dust. Where is the biographer's or autobiographer's dust best disposed? In their books, or back under the carpet? The cobwebs lie so thick it is tempting to separate out the strands, like Marge Piercy with her epigram: 'Autobiographers know everything; biographers never know enough'. It's a tidy statement. Is it just too neat?

Around the table to discuss like matters are Michael Holroyd, whose literary biographies include studies of Bernard Shaw, Augustus John and Lytton Strachey. Michael has also turned memoir writer. His sortie into family history, *Basil Street Blues* has now given rise to a sequel, *Mosaic*. Jackie Kay is quite used to transforming lives, her own and those of others, into matter for the imagination. Her novel *Trumpet* draws on the life of the American jazz musician Billy Tipton, whilst her volume of verse, *The Adoption Papers*, harks back to her own experience of adoption in 1960s Scotland. With us too is Blake Morrison, who has reconstructed the painful lives of the Yorkshire Ripper and the young murderers of James Bulger. But Blake too writes memoirs recounting his father's death in *And When Did You Last See Your Father?* [made into a film: *When Did You Last See Your Father?* 2008, dir. Anand Tucker] and his parents' courtship and marriage in *Things My Mother Never Told Me*. I incidentally am Robert Fraser and I have written a life of the twentieth century British poet George Barker, as well as plays on the lives of Dr Johnson, Lord Byron and the Renaissance princeling Carlo Gesualdo.

But to start with Michael Holroyd, this statement of Marge Piercy's: 'Autobiographers know everything; biographers never know enough', doesn't it confuse knowledge with information?

Michael Holroyd (MH): Yes, I think it does. At first gasp it sounds rather neat, and a good epigram to divide autobiographers from biographers but in fact I think biographers aren't purely after information; that's merely essential. They try and form an imaginative link with their subject in order to bring the whole person again alive on the page, whereas autobiographers would have to be, if they knew everything, miracles of memory, walking and breathing archives. I would suggest that Blake Morrison's title for the book he wrote on his mother, *Things My Mother Never Told Me*, was a far better indication of biographers' and the family memoirists' position.

RF: Remind me of the proceedings of writing a biography. We've both written biographies and you do spend a lot of time looking around in archives and in libraries and interviewing people, if people are still alive, to get the material for your book. You sometimes end up with a kind of surfeit of information, don't you?

MH: The biographer is two people, the researcher and the writer. The researcher keeps asking the writer, what do you want, and the writer says, I don't know yet, and then later on the writer says to the researcher, why didn't you get that, I needed it. You can never be sure quite what you will need; it is a voyage of discovery, and when I'm researching I long to be the writer trying to recreate, make patterns on the page. When I'm actually writing I think back with nostalgia to those wonderful days when I was travelling around like a detective finding out things, being the researcher, there's no pleasing me.

RF: Jackie, in his book *Works on Paper*, Michael quotes an aphorism of Oscar Wilde's: 'Every great man has his disciples; it is Judas who writes the biography'. In your book it's quoted as well, and the person citing it is Colman, son of the jazz trumpeter Joss Moody, who has just discovered his father was a woman. He's filled with fury at this revelation and wants to take his revenge by collaborating on a pulp tell-it-all life. It's a situation that goes to the root of biographical motivation, doesn't it?

Jackie Kay (JK): Yes I think it does. I think it's a very interesting dilemma, the dilemma between telling a life, telling a story and not telling a story. In *Trumpet* I was trying to look at old ways of telling a story, old fables and fairy tales and myth-like ways of telling a story, which seemed to me to be innocent; and then the new tabloid ugly ways of telling a story – which was going to be Colman's – because he wanted to do a kind of a kiss and tell. Colman spends a lot of his journey as a journey of redemption, a journey of acceptance where he eventually decides not to do this kiss-and-tell book because the kiss-and-tell book would have been ugly and, anyway, his father's life was kind of beautiful instead.

RF: It struck me that the title of the book, *Trumpet*, might in fact have referred to a bad biographer. That's precisely what a bad biographer does, he trumpets forth an inappropriate truth and the inappropriate truth in the case of your book is that our sexual identity is absolutely at the quick and the essence of this man. He's a much more complicated man than that but the ghost biographer who's working on the hack biography wishes to simplify him into just this problem.

JK: I think so. I think that when we try and look for a cosy or easy explanation as to why somebody does something, then we reduce them, because one single reason is never enough to explain anybody. So I never really wanted to give an answer to those questions. It seems to me that writing is all about asking questions and not answering them; I didn't want to say Joss Moody lived his life as a man because in the fifties women couldn't be jazz musicians, although that would have been part of the truth.

RF: There was a statement in your book which interested me: 'Hindsight is always a lie'. What did you mean by that?

JK: I meant that when we look back sometimes, well often, we do so in a distorted way. We have to distort things to ourselves and we do that in our own private family histories and we do it in other ways too. We don't have the benefit of hindsight while we live our lives, so when we look back with hindsight, hindsight has to be a lie.

RF: Indeed yes. Blake, in your case at least, one half of our 'motion' from Marge Piercy seemed horribly wrong. You've written about both of your parents in relation to yourself and so in that sense I suppose you're an autobiographer, and yet you had to research both books, didn't you?

Blake Morrison (BM): Yes, and I'd like to invert Marge Piercy and say, instead, that the biographer has the potential to know everything and that the autobiographer never does know very much. I say that because the autobiographer will rely on memory far more, and we know that memory is a slippery and unreliable thing, whereas the biographer potentially will have access to an archive and to a set of materials. I think that would be true of the two memoirs I've written which are part biographical, part autobiographical.

With my father I was able to stick very much to his life as it intersected with mine, so I didn't go back beyond my birth, or my childhood. I was at first having to rely on memory but, luckily, I had a notebook to reconstruct the last months of his life. I found myself asking the question as to when he was last fully alive. With my mother, writing about her, the question was: who was she? I discovered after her death that she was the nineteenth of twenty children, a fact that had never been revealed to me whilst she was alive. This seemed a fascinating aspect of her life, and also of mine. To answer that question sent me back in time, before my birth, and back to the Second World War. There was an archive of family letters, letters my father had preserved, and I was therefore able to reconstruct things that my parents were doing on a particular day in 1943, say, in immense detail. Whereas when I was relying on my memory as an autobiographer, thinking back to ten years ago and the relationship with my father, I think that would have to be partly fictional because memory is just not good or complete enough.

RF: People often oversimplify memory, don't they? You always have to impose some sort of structure on memory too. It's never a simple one-to-one relation between remembered incident and transformation. What do you think about this?

MH: Well, I'd like to take some issue here with Jackie, because I feel that hindsight is not just a lie: it is an aspect of the truth; it is an important part of the truth. In addition, the present is also, in part, a lie because it doesn't have all the implications contained in it as we come to appreciate them. It's only when you manage to join the

**95**

past with the present in some way that you can get a more rounded picture. Certain things can happen in the present, let's say they are frightening, or embarrassing, but in the past they can become comic, part of the comedy of life. Join the two together and you've got something which I think is multidimensional, and by extension is more satisfying. There one has both the awfulness and the comedy; all our lives in a sense are tragi-comedies.

JK: Absolutely, I think that's true. I think for my character hindsight was a lie because he had never been told the truth. He'd lived all of his life assuming that his father was a man, and only found out that his father was a woman after she died; so the act of going back to his past and trying to make sense of it all felt like a fabrication. Sometimes when we're given a piece of information that is new to us but that was true at the time (though we didn't know it), we do have to do that funny thing of going back and re-assessing. That activity can be very disturbing for people. In that sense I think hindsight is a lie, but of course I think all of our lives are joined together in this way; the lived present tense is never exactly the same as the actual present tense – our imagination is too powerful. For example, I was adopted. I had a very strong imaginary picture of my birth mother and my birth father, very strong indeed. When I met my real birth mother and birth father it was distressing to me because the imaginary picture had been so strong; in a way my imaginary picture of them seems to me more authentic than the real people that I met, which is an odd thing.

MH: [to Blake Morrison] Yes, in the same sense that you discovered a new mother. You knew your mother, obviously, when she was alive but what you then discovered was a new person. I mean it was a different person to some extent, you wouldn't have guessed at her nature – at least that's what I got from your book. I wondered whether that changed your perspective on your family at all and perhaps on yourself?

BM: A little. I don't feel she's completely different but yes, to discover the extent of her Irish past that she had taken pains to conceal from me, her Catholic upbringing and so forth, all suppressed when I was growing up, was a kind of revelation. Of course there's a little bit of me that, if not exactly angry with my mother, was bewildered by her. I mean, for me, to be Irish and one of twenty would be rather exotic and exciting and something to be proud of.

For my mother it was, if not a matter of shame, a matter of shyness and embarrassment and awkwardness to be played down. I felt angry on her behalf that somehow, to be assimilated into English middle-class life back in the 1940s and 50s, she had had to bury her past. Rather than being angry in the end, however, I just felt sorry that she wasn't able to be fully herself.

RF: Presumably you understood her shame ... you understood the reasons for her shame.

BM: Yes, and I think that this should be the motive of the biographer, if you like. It's a search for understanding. It's not about settling a score, it's not about taking a subject and entertainingly demolishing that subject, though we can all think of biographies that do that. It should be to provide insight, an imaginative insight, as Michael said. You know, the information itself is not enough, but we want insight, we want new ways of perceiving a famous figure or new ways of looking at very ordinary people.

RF: But in the process you're always involved in turning the private realm into the public realm and that's a difficult point of transition, isn't it? I really wanted to ask you all a related question about privacy. In Jackie's novel, Colman remembers his mother saying to him, 'Families have their own dark secrets, you never know', and in both Michael and Blake's books there's a moment when you're hovering over bundles of letters, wondering whether to open them. In Blake's case it's his parents' love letters which he's ferried down to London and after his mother's death he spends some weeks reading through them. In Michael's, it's the record of his aunt's love affair which is all the more painful because, though oblivious to what he's doing, the auntie's still alive. I wonder therefore whether life writing doesn't always involve violation of a sort?

MH: Well, I never really see biographers myself as voyeurs. I believe that if a bundle of letters has been left, there is some unconscious unresolved reason for that. Who is to say that the dead don't want messengers to tell their story when they can no longer personally be hurt, embarrassed and so on? If they leave the wherewithal for that story to be told then I think one takes the bundle and runs with it. But I very much agree with what Blake said. You mustn't feel superior to people; it is just part of the current of life, of which you are a part. The great humane lesson to be learned from biography is that we all do embarrassing things; we all do less than we should sometimes, or disreputable things. It's all part of the current, there's no 'us and them'. It's a more humane broad stream.

BM: Well, I did feel guilty for a time reading these letters, but I was also conscious that my father had kept them, shown them to me, said 'One day you'll want to read these'. He was probably not expecting me to publish them, or use them towards a book, but he did nonetheless mean me to preserve them so in a sense had given me the licence. What it comes down to, then, is your motivation, and if it's an act of – as I think it was for me and it is for many people – commemoration more than anything else, that's what matters. Go back to Horace. Horace in his *Odes* talks about lives of those 'unmourned and unknown, covered by the long night' because they didn't have their sacred poet. Well, I didn't think I was a sacred poet, but I did feel about these ordinary but interesting lives of my parents, that here's a way of commemorating them, preserving them, making them, giving them an afterlife.

RF: Jackie, you're going through this process at the moment, aren't you? You've recently been back to Nigeria looking at your Nigerian family. Are you hovering, considering problems of whether you want to bring your family's life into print?

JK: Yes, I think there is a big dilemma in what people actually want to happen. If somebody has a story that they want to be told, or if they've left a trail, like Michael and Blake were saying; if there's a bundle of letters that you come upon, then you might feel that you have some right. If people are actually alive and they're also secretive, it becomes a different dilemma. But then you've also got to ask yourself, as a writer, whose story is it? In some ways going to Nigeria meant my life seemed to be a story that was happening to me, so I have been able to write about it. My dilemma then becomes whether or not to publish it, because my father is so secretive.

BM: I think all biography tends to be thought of as an act of invasion, an act of aggression. Images of the biographer often employed include the voyeur, the exploiter; or Kipling talked about the 'higher cannibalism', so there's that very violent image too. Then, in addition, when it's a family memoir which is going to touch and affect people still living, another dimension comes in to do with ownership. For instance, Hanif Kureishi has written a fair bit about his family, and particularly his father. Every time he publishes a new book which in some way alludes to that family, you will see his sister writing to a newspaper publishing a short article disassociating herself from Hanif Kureishi's version of his family and his father. It does come down to this question of ownership, doesn't it? People feel they own lives, and of course the relations of great men and women who have appointed a biographer often feel very protective and violated when the biographer comes along.

RF: We can only really tell the relative truth, not the absolute truth.

MH: There isn't an absolute truth, there are lots of relative truths, as it were, but I think that next to the family, it is the writer who fears biography the most. It's interesting to ponder what the fear amongst other writers, dramatists, poets, novelists should be. I think they fear a sort of destabilising of their texts, the fact that everything will be reduced to autobiography, that the magic will be taken away. To this way of thinking, biographers are really fifth column agents within the ranks of writers, not to be trusted. They are dead matter like the moon, expressing no light, only reflecting light; worse, they can eclipse the sun, they can take away literary immortality. Stay clear of them, that's the message that other writers have.

BM: It is. For instance, you take somebody like Philip Larkin, and Andrew Motion's (I think terrific) biography of him, that nonetheless upset many people who did not want to know all that stuff about Larkin. They didn't want to know about his pornography habit and his gin habit and the way he treated women and so on. The fear underlying this reaction seemed to be that we would think less of the poems for knowing the fuller picture about the poet. I for one don't. I still think as much of the poems as I ever did, and I think the poems stand free. Of course there is another great fear that the writer has, that somehow the biography will be read but not the novels, not the poems, not the thing that made the life be written in the first place, that they will get ignored because the biographer has stolen the scene and the magic.

JK: Well, the life is stolen in a way, the life out of the poems, which is people's worry with, say, Sylvia Plath or Ted Hughes – that somehow, as you said, the life will eclipse the poems. I don't agree with this though. I think that our problem is that sometimes we read both the life and the work, and we then correlate one to the other in a neat way. But Sylvia Plath's poems do not necessarily tell the exact story of her life. They have an imaginative life all of their own.

MH: Yes, as you said earlier, Jackie, all our lives are of course bounded by some facts, but we also are led on by our fantasies. If you can get the two together then you've got something. But it's not just information, as we started with, it's not just information that is merely essential. It's the skeleton, yes, and you've got to bring it to life.

JK: And even a tiny piece of information, as we've all discovered, turns out not to be the piece of information that we thought it was, so then we have to even wonder what a fact is. 'Such and such is a simple fact', is a statement that must often be questioned or re-questioned or re-discovered or looked at in a different way. You might have been told a fact and you think you have this fact all of your life – but then you go back and it's not actually a fact.

MH: And also facts, even verifiable facts, can actually contradict one another. Someone can write in a diary how terrible he or she is feeling and then go out in the evening and be the life and soul of the party. Both are true but had he or she not used the diary to get rid of the poison and depression they wouldn't have been able to be the other person. A text can reconcile these contradictory positions sometimes, and it's interesting when they do.

RF: Can I move on from the private dimension of biography and autobiography towards the public dimension? Undeniably, life writing is a private act but when fully effective it always seems to possess this wider public, even sometimes political, aspect. I was very struck that at the end of both *Basil Street Blues* and *Things My Mother Never Told Me* there is the confession, a confession that what has been told has been almost a post-imperial tale. In Michael's case the decline in his family's fortunes shadows the demise of empire, and in Blake's book he takes a taxi to see his dying Irish mother; the driver is from Kashmir and Blake suddenly realises that this too is a migrant who like his mother has made a life for himself in a different country. So the book turns almost into a parable of migration, loss and recreation. And of course in Jackie's work, the political context is even clearer: it ends with Joss's father arriving from Africa. So perhaps despite its seeming solipsism, life writing always tells us as much about the world as it does about individuals?

BM: I certainly hope so. As a writer, you are only offering up your family, or your story, because you hope others will connect with it. Its public dimension, or its ability to provide moments of recognition for other people is the reason you're telling the story. The interesting dilemma I had, for instance, when I was writing the book about my father, concerned genre. I didn't know life writing existed, I didn't know quite what I was doing and I worried a great deal about dwelling on small details of domestic family life, the precise contents of my father's desk for instance. I thought, this actually could put people off, but actually it's those tiny details that draw people in. So it's private detail and it's personal detail and yet it will have a wider public dimension as well, you fervently hope.

MH: The significance of the trivial is rarely what one's after. There's also the related fact, which I hadn't realised so strongly until I got some letters from readers, that we all exist in a forest of family trees – and they interlink. These readers wrote saying things like, 'Well, you know your father's just like my uncle', and then we were off in a discussion along the lines of 'How much this story reminds me of something in my own family'. The story would be completely different of course, but nevertheless there would be an effective echo or a reflection of something. I've always rather liked that, that sense of belonging suddenly to people I'd never met or seen.

RF: Apparently Richard Dawkins, the genealogist and biologist, when he runs a postgraduate seminar in Oxford with students from all the way round the world, the first thing he does is to sit down and say, 'Well, actually everybody in this room is related'. I seem to remember that this is literally true and so I was amused on reading the sequel to *Basil Street Blues*, called *Mosaic*. In this book Michael describes the search for an individual who is a former mistress of his grandfather. He traces the roots of this woman right back to St Helens in Lancashire, where her father was thrown out of work in 1912. The individual who threw the father out of work was my great-great grandfather William Pilkington, who was running a glassworks in St Helens at the time.

MH: I wanted to ask Jackie, have you ever seen or read the Diane Middlebrook biography of Billy Tipton? Did you meet her by any chance? I ask, because I wondered how the biographer and the fiction writer would get on, and what were the different agendas you had?

JK: I have indeed read *Suits Me*, but I read it after I finished *Trumpet*, because I was provoked into writing a story around that particular theme, but I didn't really want to write about Billy Tipton. There were a couple of details that I found fascinating, but I thought that if I read a big biography then that would affect my imaginary way of trying to write about that story. I often like dealing with subjects and themes very imaginatively, though at other times I use 'reality' more explicitly. Sometimes, as well, I like to exploit the border country that exists between the two, between the ordinary and the extraordinary and the strange and the real.

RF:   But yours is also a story told with immense tact and elegance throughout, I think.

JK:   I liked the idea of keeping the protagonists' relationship private in a funny way, to try and write about them but give them also some sense of privacy, some sense of dignity. Often in our society when we talk about transvestites or transsexuals, there is a terrible loss of dignity. This discussion or commentary can have the effect of turning them into freaks, or to people that seem to not have an ordinary life, so I like showing them with their scrambled eggs on a Sunday and reading the Sunday newspapers and just having an ordinary life. It certainly seems to me as well that, as Blake and Michael were saying earlier, 'God is in the detail'. The poet W. H. Auden said something similar: and it's these little details that people relate to. Our lives in the end are not to do with whether somebody's a transsexual or a transvestite but whether somebody's experienced love, or experienced grief and all these things are common to all of us.

RF:   I remember a phrase that constantly plucked at my elbow when I was writing about George Barker was 'the morality of style'. It seemed to me how I told it made all the difference to the way that the story was received both by myself and others and the Barker family.

JK:   [To Blake Morrison] I'm very interested in the whole business of structure, because it seems to me that really good biographies are very tense and thrilling reads. Conversely, those that are not so good, they're saggy and they're dead. Structure is the key to success in some ways, then, and by structure I don't necessarily mean a chronological structure. How do you arrive at the structure? Is it a door that opens to you as if by magic, or how do you find it by other means?

BM: Well, I do think it is a matter of finding it almost by accident, and not knowing what it's going to be. For instance, the structure that came to dominate *When Did You Last See Your Father?* involved moving between the present tense of my father dying, and going into the past, going into my childhood, my adolescence. Always, though, the concern was with my search for the real man and where he was in the story. That seemed to evolve naturally; it wasn't a structure I would have hit upon, not a structure I could have planned ahead. And it evolved partly as a way of maintaining an element of suspense, I think. When I was telling the story of my parents I of course wanted the book, as Jackie was saying above, to have narrative suspense. The big question of the book was: would they be able to marry? The book unfolds all the obstacles that could prevent them from marrying, but obviously I'm there to write the book, and I'm the son of these two people. It's clear that they are going to marry (or at least to have a child), and yet I wanted to try to keep that narrative momentum, and some degree of suspense. So, yes, this matter of structure is terribly important.

MH: It seems to me to be a balance between a sort of historical perspective and detachment, and an absolute involvement. If you have just involvement it becomes too sentimental; if you have just the historical perspective, it's dry as dust. It's that tightrope you have to walk.

RF: Jackie, you have written poetry which has got an autobiographical base, so presumably you were faced with a different problem of transformation: how to turn memory into poetry. Can you talk a bit about this?

JK: Yes, it was in my first book, *The Adoption Papers*, where I wrote in three different voices: the birth mother, the adoptive mother, and the daughter. It was interesting when I was writing it, talking about inventing yourself, because the daughter's voice was, in fact, the most difficult to write. Both the mothers were comparatively easy to find a voice for; the daughter I found more difficult – and this was because she was, in a way, trying to tell the factual story. I realised I found that aspect less imaginative and therefore less easy to create – this was a surprising part of the project. I did also want to create three very different voices. The adoptive mother's voice is very down-to-earth and practical, and the birth mother's voice is more ethereal because I wanted to show that, in a sense, I was giving birth to her. She was part of my imagination; I hadn't met her at the time that I wrote these poems so I didn't want her voice to be down-to-earth or real. For me, above all, *The Adoption Papers* was to do with voice and tone and trying to get those characters' voices right; my own part was a character too, I didn't want to write it as though it were straight autobiography.

In a sense, then, I wanted it to tell a 'multi-story', because that's what it seems to me adoption is. This is noteworthy for me, because my biggest worry about that book was that it was going to be self-indulgent. I remember my dad, my adoptive dad, saying, 'Are you not on a wee bit of a trip for yourself here?' And I really did worry about this, but in the event many adopted people, or birth mothers of adopted people, have written to me since its publication, expressing their identification with the ideas raised by the book. (It's astounding the amount of people that either are adopted, or know of some secret about adoption.) Adoption is something very, very personal but this just shows you that when you do write something that you think is deeply personal to you, it's often not actually. Everything deeply personal to you will have its echoes in others; just like Michael was saying with the forest of trees, the families and the forest of trees, there will be lots of us that have the same experience.

BM: I suppose one could say that autobiography is going to be about providing recognition of ordinariness, whereas biography, still, we still tend to think of as being concerned with the lives of extra-ordinary people. That's why we want to read them, but we read memoirs, on the other hand, because we hope to find some connection with ourselves. Another qualification I'd want to make (rather like I wanted to invert Marge Piercy) regards the idea that auto-biographies are somehow self-absorbed and egomaniac, whereas biographies are self-effacing and the writer disappears. I don't think this is always, or even often, the case. We can all think of biographers who intrude quite a lot, for example Peter Ackroyd will 'come into' his biographies. Some biographers even might be said to over-intrude. But we can also think of rather modest, self-effacing autobiographers. I'd say that Michael, who indeed is sitting here, is sort of quiet in his memoirs. There's not too much self-inflation going on there. So the two forms are not, in their individual ways, it seems to me, always about either vanity or modesty. There are all sorts of different ways that one can write biography or autobiography.

JK:   It is a worry, though, as we have been saying, when you set out to write about your life or anything real to you. I think there is a genuine worry as to how it will relate to other people and whether other people will find it interesting. Your hope is of course that they really will.

RF:   Can I ask you one last question about structure? It's about loose threads, because there must be a point when the book clicks, you think 'it's done, the structure's right, I've got the balance right'. Yet I notice that all of you in your books leave loose threads. There are plenty of threads left untied in Joss Moody's story and Blake, you leave the question of whether you have unacknowledged half-siblings hanging in both of your books. Michael, in your turn there's your quest for Agnes May, the mistress of your grandfather whose last portrait you haven't quite tracked down. Do you think maybe that incompleteness is part of a satisfying form?

MH:   I certainly think that, yes. It's almost a metaphor for immortality, or things without end. But I think that it also shows that we do not know everything, we shouldn't pretend to know everything, there are always loose ends in our own lives. This is part of the excitement and interest of life.

RF:   What do you think, Jackie?

JK:   I think that in *Trumpet* I wanted to leave spaces (another way of imagining 'loose threads'), a bit like the silence that you get in jazz music. If you didn't have particular pauses in music, the piece of music would be a different piece of music. The silence and the pauses in music are just as important as the notes.

RF:   And Blake?

BM:   Well, yes, I think biography, autobiography, they're about truth but the truth is people are elusive, and contradictory, as we have been discussing. You want, in the end, to be able to acknowledge that, so you would hope that, by devoting a book to a subject, you and the reader will come to understand that person better. But it's also necessary to signal that there is quite a bit about them that you haven't managed to fathom. They're still elusive, and that's perfectly alright, as you will never either know or understand the whole story.

JK:   It's just like when you are adopted, and you decide to trace people, because you think that by tracing people you will understand something crucial about yourself. Actually you don't. All you discover is that this isn't the case; there isn't any kind of neat tying, there isn't any proper end of story. All there is is an unfolding of a new story.

MH: And indeed there's no such thing as a definitive biography.

RF: I think we have agreed that neither the biographer nor the auto-biographer is omniscient.

In conclusion, I hope we haven't left too many loose threads, but have provided fodder both for foresight and hindsight. Thank you, Michael, thank you, Jackie and thank you, Blake.

## Activity 6.1   Writing

Now make some notes of what you considered to be the most useful or interesting aspects of this discussion. What stood out as a new way of thinking about writing? Which techniques described by these well-known authors do you most want to try out in your own writing? Keep your response to this last question to hand as you move into the second half of the book, and refer to it as you attempt the activities there.

## References

Fraser, Robert (2002) *The Chameleon Poet: A life of George Barker*, London: Pimlico.

Hind, Angela (producer) (2005) round table discussion, A215 *Creative Wtiting* CD3, 'Life Writing', Milton Keynes: The Open University/Pier Productions.

Holroyd, Michael (1999) *Basil Street Blues: A memoir*, London: Norton.

Holroyd, Michael (2002) *Works On Paper: The craft of biography and autobiography*, London: Little, Brown & Co.

Holroyd, Michael (2004) *Mosaic: A family memoir revisited*, London: Little, Brown & Co.

Kay, Jackie (1991) *The Adoption Papers*, London: Learning Links.

Kay, Jackie (1998) *Trumpet*, London: Picador.

Middlebrook, Diane (1999) *Suits Me: The double life of Billy Tipton*, New York: Houghton Mifflin.

Morrison, Blake (1993) *And When Did You Last See Your Father?: A son's memoir of love and loss*, London: Granta.

Morrison, Blake (2002) *Things My Mother Never Told Me*, London: Chatto and Windus.

Motion, Andrew (1993) *Philip Larkin: A writer's life*, New York: Farrar, Strauss & Giroux.

# 7

# Using memory

*Derek Neale*

## Remembering lives

When a life story is composed rival versions of that life often arise, as you have seen in the discussion of the previous chapter. There may be no possibility of a definitive biography, and yet the writer is driven to pin down some sort of truth. We will be addressing the issue of different testimonies and how to incorporate them in your projects in the next chapter. In this chapter we will investigate how memory might be used, given its fallible status. As Blake Morrison stated, memory is 'a slippery and unreliable thing' and often lies at the centre of any controversy about how a life might be described. Yet memory is crucially important to biography and autobiography. In both the writer is recalling in complex fashion the habits, relationships and cultural setting of a life.

In the opening chapters of this book you were shown the advantages to be gained from using memory and details of your everyday world in your life writing. It is also important to be aware that biography and autobiography aren't necessarily exclusive categories. The writers' testimonies in the last chapter attested that when writing of your own life you will often find yourself writing about the lives of other people – you might want to give outlines of your father's or mother's life history, for instance, or you may wish to detail the daily routine of a friend. On the other hand, when concerned with a biographical subject, one that doesn't have a personal link to your life, you might like to include yourself in the narrative, as many modern journalists do in magazine interviews and articles, and as some writers of biography also do.

It has already been mentioned that life writing doesn't necessarily have to follow a straightforward, start-to-finish chronology; you don't have to begin your narrative with a birth and end either with a death or in your subject's old age. The beginning of Dickens's *David Copperfield* is just one approach. For instance, you might just focus on a fixed period of time. Consider the start of J.D. Salinger's *Catcher in the Rye*, for the antithesis of Dickens's beginning:

> If you really want to hear about it, the first thing you'll probably want to know is where I was born, and what my lousy childhood was like, and how my parents were occupied and all before they had me, and all that David Copperfield kind of crap, but I don't feel like going into it, if you want to know the truth. In the first place, that stuff bores me ... I'm not going to tell you my whole goddam autobiography or anything. I'll just tell you about this madman stuff that happened to me around last Christmas just before I got pretty run-down and had to come out here and take it easy.
>
> (Salinger 1994 [1951]: 1)

As with *David Copperfield*, this is the beginning of a novel, but it seems to be using and commenting upon the conventions of autobiography. It includes the reader, a second person addressee, as part of the narrative and establishes the boundaries of personal experience to be dealt with in the narrative; the memory is going to be finite. Also, two most pertinent points are made about the relationship between writer and subject matter: if you're writing about a life it is important not to be bored, and to inhabit the conventions of the genre in a personal fashion. Treat life writing like a bespoke garment, tailor-made for your subject matter, rather than something you've bought off the shelf which you have to fit into.

In this way your content will define the form of your writing. It can be a poem with little narrative, for instance, based around the memory of a moment; or it can be a dramatic scene involving many characters. As Richard Holmes says, 'Why should the biographer be limited to one kind of narrative voice, one kind of discursive prose?' (Holmes 2000: xi). His book *Sidetracks* includes pieces that are biography and autobiography, and which take the form of radio plays, travel writing, essays, character-sketches, and short stories. All of them were 'written as different ways of investigating biographical material' (Holmes 2000: xi). In this call for the use of various narrative methods Holmes echoes the approach of Ruth Picardie and Susanna Kaysen, mentioned in Chapters 4 and 5. The suggestion is that your narrative voice and form will always arise from your purpose and the area of personal or biographical experience you are writing about.

## Using your memory

Remember the advice offered in Chapters 1 and 2: think of memory as something that you can use to enrich your writing, not something you should feel obliged to adhere to. Recall as well the passage from *Catcher in the Rye*: if you are bored by an over-rehearsed episode from your past, then the chances are your reader will be bored too. You will need to reinvigorate it. The episode might be the first day in a new job, for instance, when you spilt a cup of coffee over yourself and felt embarrassed. You can revive the memory by looking at it from a different perspective perhaps; imagine a colleague watching what was happening. Ask some pertinent questions: who else was there? What sort of day was it? What were you wearing? Did you like the job? Who did you speak to on that first day? Asking questions like these, and answering just some of them while inventing answers to others (it would be impossible to remember all such details), is the way to revive the scene and events, for you and for your reader.

Looking back over your own life may flush out uncomfortable memories. The purpose of investigating your own life in these chapters is not necessarily therapeutic, though it may throw up therapeutic benefits. The activities are designed to improve your writing, not to spark wholesale re-evaluations of your life. If you find some of the autobiographical exercises too taxing or disturbing, it might be an idea to concentrate on biographical writing or a different era of your life.

When writing about your own life you will be calling on both your associative memory and your narrative memory, as discussed in Chapter 1. For instance, with a train of associative recall about the coffee incident you might think of flowers in a vase on one of the desks; the office and the type of work you did in the job; the big windows looking out onto the street; a painted brick wall on your route to work and a garage on the corner of the road and the smell of petrol; the mole on a colleague's forehead; another colleague, soon to become a friend, helping you to clean up the coffee and kindly pouring you another cup; perhaps you remember the friend's first name but can't recall more. These thoughts would all come in quick succession, and in no specific order.

With the second type of recall – narrative memory – you will have a less unruly train of thought. Events will be ordered in a time sequence, so you have in effect formed a story of events in your mind. You go to work on your first day and during the morning break you are drinking coffee and talking about the holiday you've just been on. A wasp comes in through the window and, in trying to avoid it, you spill your coffee. A colleague helps you to clean up, but for the rest of the day you feel clumsy and are conscious of the stain on your clothes.

Now let's try to get both kinds of memory – associative and narrative – working.

### Activity 7.1   Writing

Draw a circle in the centre of a page in your notebook and in it write the word 'yesterday'. Create a cluster of associations, by writing down all the words and phrases that you can think of to do with what happened to you yesterday. Do this as rapidly as you can, circling each word and linking it back to this central word – 'yesterday'. Some words may have direct links, others may have indirect links. In doing this you will create a visual map of your thoughts.

When you have finished, on a separate page write a single sentence about what happened to you yesterday.

### Discussion

These are two quite different ways of recalling your life. Writing the sentence meant that you had to arrange the words according to the conventions of grammar, so that they were being organised into some sort of sequence. While composing it you might also have thought of new words to put over in the associative cluster. On reflection the sentence might seem reductive as a version of the day, especially in comparison with the cluster version. Yet the cluster isn't entirely comprehensible to a reader, maybe not even to you; this too may seem dissatisfying as a version of the day. It will be important to harness and integrate both types of recall when writing about your life: to arrange your thoughts and memories as a narrative when needed, so that events appear in a time sequence with settings, characters and causalities; but also to capture the spontaneity of associative and resonant ways of remembering. Each way of remembering on its own may not provide a complete enough picture.

This is a useful exercise to return to, or to start a project. You might like to try it with different focuses. For instance:

- looking in the mirror and using your reflection;
- using an old photograph of yourself.

It is a useful exercise for writing biography as well as autobiography. When you are writing about another person's life you will need to make the most of all possible perceptions of that person. Try:

- a photograph of a friend or relative;
- a photograph of a celebrity you like;
- a photograph of a celebrity you dislike.

## Storied lives

People's lives and their memories of those lives often read like constructed narratives, stories that have been in some way crafted. That is not to say that they are artificial; it is just a reflection of the fact that stories are a common way in which we actively think about and preserve our pasts. It is a pattern of thinking and representation we fall into even when we are attempting to be scientific, as Freud says about his patients' case studies:

> Like other neuropathologists, I was trained to employ local diagnoses and electro-prognosis, and it still strikes me myself as strange that the case histories I write should read like short stories [. . .] I must console myself with the reflection that the nature of the subject is evidently responsible for this, rather than any preference of my own.
>
> (Freud 1955: 160)

When the 'subject' is someone's life history, their sensibility and familial relationships, any representation is likely to resemble a story. Any attempt to remember all or part of a life involves ordering fragments, an editorial process of inclusion and exclusion, similar to the one you've just gone through with the cluster and the sentence. As Graham Greene says, 'An autobiography is only "a sort of life" – it may contain less errors of fact than a biography, but it is of necessity even more selective' (Greene 1974 [1971]: 9). Memories are a form of fiction-making and storytelling, and there is a fundamental difference between living a life and recalling that life.

Jean-Paul Sartre's novel *Nausea* is written in the form of a journal. Its narrator, Roquentin, states his intention on the first page:

> . . . to write down everything that happens from day to day. To keep a diary in order to understand. To neglect no nuances or little details, even if they seem unimportant . . .
>
> (Sartre 1963: 9)

The premise of the novel is a metaphysical exploration of the discrepancies between living a life and recounting that life, either in thought and memory or in writing. Roquentin from time to time comes to some conclusions:

> . . . for the most commonplace event to become an adventure, you must – and this is all that is necessary – start *recounting* it. This is what fools people: a man is always a teller of tales, he lives surrounded by his stories and the stories of others, he sees everything that happens to him through them; and he tries to live his life as if he were recounting it.
>
> (Sartre 1963: 61)

This observation – that we think of our lives as stories – is most important when coming to write biography and autobiography. If writers like Sartre, Dickens and Salinger seem to be using the conventions of life writing in their novels, the reverse is also true. As Michael Holroyd says:

> Biographers have learned a good deal from novelists – even from the writers of detective stories and thrillers. Though the biographer may not invent dialogue, he may use short quotations from letters and diaries, poetry and prose, which have the immediacy of dialogue.
>
> (Holroyd 2002: 26)

Even the contention here, that the biographer can't use the fictional technique of writing dialogue as if recalled verbatim, has been challenged. In many of the examples of life writing that you will look at, dialogue is used to illustrate both typical and specific exchanges between characters. Also, the use of the third person, a technique which would seem only suited to fiction or biographical writing, can also be used in autobiographical writing, as shown in such texts as Paul Auster's *The Invention of Solitude*, specifically the second part, 'The Book of Memory' (Auster 1988 [1982]: 71ff.). Auster describes how he eventually came to use the third person:

> When I started the next section, I assumed it would be written in the first person as well. I worked on it for six or eight months in that form but something wasn't right [. . .] What it came down to was creating a distance between myself and myself. If you're too close to the thing you're trying to write about, the perspective vanishes, and you begin to smother. I had to objectify myself in order to explore my own subjectivity.
>
> (Auster 1996: 147)

This is another instance of life experience being revived by using a certain writing technique. Auster's novels and autobiographical writing are all concerned with exploring the 'shape of a life' (Auster 2004). For him lives are not scientific entities that can be easily verified. The recall of lives is a subjective affair, and often for the reader it is this personal regard for the past which holds the intrinsic appeal. Memory might be fallible but it is based on experience, a consciousness of life which is littered with elements that seem to offer themselves up as undeniably true. For instance, there is the sensory recall surrounding an event. As seen with the Proust example in Chapter 1, a smell or sound will sometimes be the trigger. Sometimes it will present itself as evidence of the truth of a memory. This is the case with Graham Greene, talking about his boyhood hide-away:

> The danger of discovery lent those hours a quality of excitement which was very close to momentary happiness. Scent to me is far more evocative than sound or perhaps even sight, so that I become attracted without realizing it to the smell of a floor-polish or a detergent which one day I miss when I open my door and home

seems no longer home. So in my sixties I seem able to smell the leaves and grasses of my hiding-place more certainly than I hear the dangerous footsteps on the path or see the countryman's boots pass by on the level of my eyes.

(Greene 1974 [1971]: 56)

Here the sensory faculties seem to be governing the memory, and the emotional colour of the events is given priority over their sequence in time, their causality and arrangement into the form of a story.

## Author interview

Some of Jenny Diski's novels have obvious autobiographical elements and her memoirs, *Skating to Antarctica* (1998 [1997]) and *Stranger on a Train* (2004 [2002]), can be read both as travel narratives and as explorations of her own past. I met up with her for a recorded Open University interview. The following is an edited extract from the interview, and offers some detailed insight into how Diski goes about writing of her own life. As you are reading, note what Diski says about:

- the relationship between memory and writing;
- the differences between writing fiction and autobiography;
- her methods for collecting conversations and interviews.

Jenny Diski (JD): *Skating to Antarctica* was written immediately after I wrote *The Dream Mistress* which was a novel and it covered very similar ground and in a way I think of them as companion volumes and I had, as it were, both books in mind. I knew I was going to be writing *Skating* when I wrote *Dream Mistress* so they're very linked and part of the fun of writing it was playing around with the same material and playing around with fiction and non-fiction.

Derek Neale (DN): But when writing about your own life, you're obviously writing about things that actually happened?

JD: Well, I don't know if I'm writing about things that actually happened, either in fiction or non-fiction. What I'm dealing with, I suppose specifically in non-fiction – although I'd say the same thing about fiction – is memory. I'm not sure that memory and imagination aren't so inextricably linked as to be much the same thing. So I'm talking, I suppose, about real things in my background. On the other hand we're talking about things sometimes that were decades ago, so how I remember them is pretty much how I imagine them and I'm quite interested in that. I mean in *Skating* for example, I pictured myself being somewhere and it seems to me that is very much more to do with imagination, if you like, than what people strictly think of as memory, so that's part of the sort of investigation.

DN: There's a version of memory in *Skating to Antarctica* which is to do with memory as storytelling. I just wonder whether you could elaborate on that a little?

JD: Well, my guess is how we build memory or long-term memory is by telling ourselves stories. I've certainly watched it in children, my own daughter and so on. When something strong happens it has to be retold back to them as a story, over and over and over again. The story seems sort of central because it exists in time and we exist in time and so long as there's a past, present and a future we're going to need to make sense of events in that way. Memory is really stuff that's happened to us that we've made sense of by turning it into a story, just as we do with dreams. The idea of [*Skating to Antarctica* was], 'Oh, I'm gonna write about going to Antarctica because I want to go to Antarctica', and my mother because some little bulb lit up and I thought, 'Oh, mothers and glaciers and icebergs.' A book requires a structure; structure requires a story. Part of the story is extremely easy because by definition a travel of some sort is a story; you start somewhere and you end up somewhere.

I think I'm not interested in travel writing as such. I'm really not interested in going somewhere and then coming back to tell people about it because I can't understand why they don't go there themselves or they don't watch it on telly. They'd be much better off letting David Attenborough do it for them and, I don't know, getting a can of penguin pee to smell if you really want it to be authentic. On the other hand I did want to go somewhere and I wanted to write white, so that's the point, the point was, 'I want to write about ice and snow and white and emptiness', but it's all about making that kind of choice. I wanted to bounce some things that I'd been writing about off what you might call reality.

DN: So potentially you could write a narrative about a bus journey?

JD: Yes, absolutely and I have done, I mean, I've written long essays about doing almost nothing and in fact for a year I was the supermarket correspondent for the *Sunday Times* and did 350 words a week on my visit to the supermarket which was sublime really because in fact all human life is there. If you're writing 350 words a week on going to the supermarket and you go to the supermarket, you find you have at least 350 words to write. It's really not a problem and the truth is you can write about anything at all, of course you can. I'd like to do a thing I think for radio, just going and sitting in places in Kings Cross for the day and then reporting back. And it's not about what's happening out there and about the drama of out there; it's to do with the interaction I suppose of what's going on in your head and what's happening out there. I'm really only interested in what goes on in my head but I put my head in slightly different venues sometimes, that's all.

DN: Why did you want to write about white?

JD: I don't know. I wanted really to write about being in a completely empty white room which is sort of how I conceived of Antarctica and why I wanted to go there. I mean, what is it you want when you go somewhere? Well, I wanted this kind of blank whiteness, not that I could have possibly got it. That's the other thing about travel writing; you know the only interesting travel writing it seems to me is disappointment, not getting what you think you're going to get but being surprised and interrupted in your expectations. So that the conscious notion was I wanted to write about white. I'm hardly the first person to do it. Melville of course has an entire chapter on white in *Moby Dick*. That's actually one of my favourite books; it's a book I sort of keep going back to and actually I read as well again on that trip. And then of course there's accident. Within the two concepts saying, 'Let's stick my mother and Antarctica together', there is the accident of what looks as if it's the basis of the story and it is the basis of the book. Which is that my daughter wanted to see if her grandmother was alive. And it happened just about the same time. So off I went back to Paramount Court [where Diski lived when growing up] and found, lo and behold, that these extremely old ladies were still sitting there that had been there when I was a child.

DN: Meeting your old neighbours – part of that you script as if it was in a play, did you record that dialogue, or is it a fictional representation?

JD: Well – the old ladies who eventually I came to conceive of as a kind of semi-Greek chorus or chorus girls – in fact I recorded those conversations and they're verbatim. I recorded them and I typed them all up and I didn't change anything, I mean I edited stuff obviously, I didn't put in every single conversation, but the words [in the book] are the words that are used. Obviously they knew I was taping them and I had specific things I wanted to ask. That was all very journalistic. On the trips, for example on the boat trip to Antarctica, I didn't do any of that. When I'm travelling I don't, I just do a kind of journal – that's putting it too formally really, but I just make notes in the evening or whenever I get back to my cabin about anything in particular that's happened. And then what I write up is pretty much how I remember it, which of course is entirely inaccurate.

For *Stranger*, the BBC sent me off with a big microphone, you know one of those fuzzy things on them, and I just schlepped this thing around. You know it was really heavy, and the first sort of conversation I had I thought about getting it out. But it was insane, you know you can't sit on a train in a smoky compartment and stick a microphone in someone's face and say 'Let's have an easy conversation'. So I never did. What I do is tell everybody that I'm a writer and that I'm writing about the journey and then I have conversations and then I write them down, so everybody knows that I'm going to be, or may be, writing down what we say. Clearly it's not accurate because when I sent *Stranger* to the editors in America and asked them to check it, they came back because somebody used the word 'trousers' which of course no American ever uses; they say 'pants'. So, it's a translation is what it is. I do want the characters to be as close as I can get them to real, as close as I can get them to the texture of who they were when I met them. It's partly because I owe them something; they're real and I've made them, but they're not mine, as it were.

DN: I think you say somewhere in *Stranger on a Train* how all lives seem stereotypical in some way, and your first representation of all these characters seems to actually hit on how big they are, where they come from or some typical feature; and then the character grows from that.

JD: Well, I don't know that I've got a plan about it, but it is of course how people present themselves. On the whole what happens if

**119**

you're sitting next to someone on a train is that they say where they've come from because where they've come from and where they're going is the central fact about them, you know, it's the conduit really; it's what connects all of us. We're all from somewhere and we're all going somewhere. That's how people introduce themselves. It's simply the way the community [on the train] existed actually and even on the boat really. We were all going to the same place but we were all from different places and that was a sort of distinction. It seems to me that human life goes in some pretty basic ways and what people want to tell you about when they're strangers is how unhappy they are or what they do for a living or how their children are. None of us are linking up for life, almost by definition. We're glancing off each other and when you glance off the world, what you get are essential stories.

DN: Do you think you protect anybody when you're writing about them, do you hide identities?

JD: The elderly ladies in *Skating* specifically said they wanted me to change their names, I'm not sure why really, so I did, of course. Obviously I change people's names unless I've discussed with them otherwise. I tend to change descriptions. The problem is that so very often people are so essentially what they are that it makes you want to weep to change things. People look in a particular way, or even their names sometimes are so perfect. You change things only because you absolutely have to. I change as little as I possibly can.

You can see from Diski's testimony that she sees writing about her own life to be made up of various different kinds of writing – it is sometimes like writing stories, sometimes like writing journalism. What she savours most is the detail about the characters and setting, and the traces of memory that give her a vivid sense of a past life. Yet she is also very honest and illuminating about how difficult, and often impossible, it is to attain the sort of veracity of detail that is associated with 'real life' narratives. She talks of the process as being one of translation rather than one of straightforward recording. However, she sees admitting to this difficulty, and the consequent recourse to using the imagination in order to reconstruct events, as both inevitable and peculiarly more truthful. We will now consider this further.

## Activity 7.2   Reading

Read over two items you looked at in Chapter 1:

- the extract from *Cider with Rosie* by Laurie Lee;
- Seamus Heaney's poem 'Death of a Naturalist'.

Then read the following two extracts from Hilary Mantel's memoir *Giving up the Ghost*. In your notebook detail the different ways in which a memory of sensory perceptions is at work in these writings. What 'associative' detail is being noted? How is the memory being ordered into story form?

### from *Giving up the Ghost*

In the February of 2002, my godmother Maggie fell ill, and hospital visits took me back to my native village. After a short illness she died, at the age of almost ninety-five, and I returned again for her funeral. I had been back many times over the years, but on this occasion there was a particular route I had to take: down the winding road between the hedgerows and the stone wall, and up a wide unmade track which, when I was small, people called 'the carriage drive'. It leads uphill to the old school, now disused, then to the convent, where there are no nuns these days, then to the church. When I was a child this was my daily walk, once in the morning to school and once again to school after dinner – that meal which the south of England calls lunch. Retracing it as an adult, in my funeral black, I felt a sense of oppression, powerful and familiar. Just before the public road joins the carriage drive came a point where I was overwhelmed by fear and dismay. My eyes moved sideways, in dread, towards dank vegetation, tangled bracken: I wanted to say, stop here, let's go no further. I remembered how when I was a child, I used to think I might bolt, make a run for it, scurry back to the (comparative) safety of home. The point where fear overcame me was the point of no turning back.

(Mantel 2003: 21)

I have an investment in accuracy; I would never say, 'It doesn't matter, it's history now.' I know, on the other hand, that a small child has a strange sense of time, where a year seems a decade, and everyone over the age of ten seems grown-up and of an equal age;

so although I feel sure of what happened, I am less sure of the sequence and the dateline. I know, too, that once a family has acquired a habit of secrecy, memories begin to distort, because its members confabulate to cover the gaps in the facts; you have to make some sort of sense of what's going on around you, so you cobble together a narrative as best you can. You add to it, and reason about it, and the distortions breed distortions.

Still, I think people can remember: a face, a perfume: one true thing or two. Doctors used to say babies didn't feel pain; we know they were wrong. We are born with our sensibilities; perhaps we are conceived that way. Part of our difficulty in trusting ourselves is that in talking of memory we are inclined to use geological metaphors. We talk about buried parts of our past and assume the most distant in time are the hardest to reach: that one has to prospect for them with the help of a hypnotist, or psychotherapist. I don't think memory is like that: rather that it is like St Augustine's 'spreading limitless room'. Or a great plain, a steppe, where all the memories are laid side by side, at the same depth, like seeds under the soil.

There is a colour of paint that doesn't seem to exist any more, that was a characteristic pigment of my childhood. It is a faded, rain-drenched crimson, like stale and drying blood. You saw it on panelled front doors, and on the frames of sash windows, on mill gates and on those high doorways that led to the ginnels between shops and gave access to their yards. You can still see it, on the more soot-stained and dilapidated old buildings, where the sand-blaster hasn't yet been in to turn the black stone to honey: you can detect a trace of it, a scrape. The restorers of great houses use paint scrapes to identify the original colour scheme of old salons, drawing rooms and staircase halls. I use this paint scrape – oxblood, let's call it – to refurbish the rooms of my childhood: which were otherwise dark green, and cream, and more lately a cloudy yellow, which hung about at shoulder height, like the aftermath of a fire.

(Mantel 2003: 24–5)

### Discussion

As seen earlier, 'Death of a Naturalist' is full of sensory perception and seems to be composed of the associative memories from many occasions. Yet it also settles down into one specific time. Similarly, the *Cider with Rosie* extract is full of sensory detail based on memory; the detail accumulates effortlessly to realise time, place and event. Mantel's narrative is more self-conscious. Whereas Lee's passage confidently integrates the two kinds of recall, narrative and associative, Mantel directly addresses the issue of how the reality of past events is difficult to ascertain. First of all she admits the contemporary position from which the recollection is being made, by revisiting the 'carriage drive' as an adult and revealing what habitually rather than specifically happened to her as a child. She goes on to talk about the unreliability of memory and how she is unsure of the dateline, while describing the most vivid sensory recalls.

### Activity 7.3    Writing

Think of a place from your past (not necessarily your childhood, it could be from your more recent past) – it might be a room, a street, or a garden, but not necessarily any of these. You choose. Spend ten minutes listing things about the place or creating a cluster for it in your notebook.

Then either write 250 words or write a 16-line poem about the place. Whether writing prose or poetry, use sensory detail, creating a sense of many occasions, but also situating yourself there at a certain time, possibly with other characters. For example, you might write about a field where you regularly played with your friends as a child; you might remember the smell of the newly cut grass and recall an occasion when you hurt yourself when playing there. Alternatively, it could be a street where you had to catch the bus to work, how the bus shelter smelt of stale cigarette smoke, and how you once saw an old friend in the queue.

### *Discussion*

When you have finished, reflect for a moment on whether you have gained any new insight or had to invent any detail in order to write about the recall. The process of writing can often enrich a memory; detail can arise just from trying to focus on an event.

### Unreliable memories

As Mantel indicates, memory is notoriously susceptible to suggestion. For instance, the Swiss psychologist Jean Piaget had a vivid memory from when he was a very young child, of his nursery nurse being attacked by an assailant while walking him in the park. This memory of the event stayed with him for many years. He was convinced by the detail of the memory, even though he was only in a pram at the time. The nurse was awarded a watch as some sort of compensation for the ordeal. Years later the nurse returned the watch, saying she'd made the whole thing up. Piaget had believed the nurse's story so thoroughly that he'd invented images to go with it, yet it was an incident that never took place (Piaget 1951: 187–8).

Certain memories will be clear to you and seem undeniably true; others will be shrouded in doubt. You may suspect some parts of your recall to be influenced by other people, or to be altered by the passage of time. Some narratives, like that from *Cider with Rosie*, admit less doubt; the dramatisation is presented as fact despite Lee being so young at the time. Mantel's approach is more circumspect, as you can see as she proceeds.

## Activity 7.4  Reading

Read this later extract from *Giving up the Ghost* below.

In your notebook identify the parts that are influenced by suggestion or which acknowledge the power of suggestion. What narrative techniques are being used to present the recall?

### From *Giving up the Ghost*

This is the first thing I remember. I am sitting up in my pram. We are outside, in the park called Bankswood. My mother walks backwards. I hold out my arms because I don't want her to go. She says she's only going to take my picture. I don't understand why she goes backwards, back and aslant, tacking to one side. The trees overhead make a noise of urgent conversation, too quick to catch; the leaves part, the sky moves, the sun peers down at me. Away and away she goes, till she comes to a halt. She raises her arm and partly hides her face. The sky and trees rush over my head. I feel dizzied. The entire world is sound, movement. She moves towards me, speaking. The memory ends.

This memory exists now in black and white, because when I was older I saw Bankswood pictures: this photograph or similar ones, perhaps taken that day, perhaps weeks earlier, or weeks later. In the nineteen-fifties photographs often didn't come out at all, or were so fuzzy that they were thrown away. What remains as a memory, though the colour has bled away, is the fast scudding of clouds and the rush of sound over my head, the wind in the trees: as if the waters of life have begun to flow.

Many years later, when there was a suspicion about my heart, I was sent to hospital for a test called an echocardiogram. A woman rolled me with a big roller. I heard the same sound, the vast, pulsing, universal roar: my own blood in my own veins. But for a time I didn't know whether that sound came from inside me, or from the depth of the machines by my bed.

I am learning, always learning. To take someone's picture, you move away from them. When you have finished, you move back.

The results of the test, I should say, were satisfactory. My heart was no bigger than one would expect.

I learn to walk in the house, but don't remember that. Outside the house, you turn left: I don't know it's left. Moving towards the next-door house: from my grandmother (56 Bankbottom, Hadfield, Near Manchester) to her elder sister, at no. 58. Embedded in the stonework on the left of my grandmother's door is a rusty iron ring. I always slip my finger into it, though I should not. Grandad says it is where they tied the monkey up, but I don't think they really ever had one; all the same, he lurks in my mind, a small grey monkey with piteous eyes and a long active tail.

(Mantel 2003: 27–8)

### Discussion

The memory of Bankswood seems to have been created by the photographs of that location seen at a later age. The photographs have helped create the scene of the photo shoot. Mantel's narrative acknowledges how the combination of fact and fiction is working, but this doesn't undermine the veracity of the account, in fact it adds to it. The vivid detail of the 'fast scudding clouds and the rush of sound over my head, the wind in the trees' combines with a later sensibility that can say 'as if the waters of life have begun to flow', and is also informed by the black and white photos of the 1950s. In this way memories are never a reflection solely of their moment of inception; they are continually influenced by different eras in their protagonist's life.

Mantel's narrative is structured in relatively short, sharp bursts of information, co-ordinated around certain recurring features – such as the narrator's age, and the numbers of certain houses which are key locations in her childhood. Such methods create fragments which are linked by a not necessarily continuous through-line. Each burst narrates a concerted episode and seems almost self-contained; it isn't continuous with the preceding or subsequent passages. Yet later when, for instance, a house number recurs, the narrative connection is made between different passages. The use of the present tense lends the narrative immediacy; it declares to the reader that, although it is happening in the past, this narrative is coming from the present, the writer is still investigating the episode.

## Imagination and memory

As Philip Roth says, 'the facts are never just coming at you but are incorporated by an imagination that is formed by your previous experience. Memories of the past are memories not of facts but memories of your imaginings of the facts' (Roth 1988: 8). Imagination can play a big part in any reconstruction of events, as suggested by Jenny Diski and also suggested in Chapter 4, in Ford Madox Ford's approach to writing the biography of Joseph Conrad. Personal impressions are an important form of information about a life, but they are notoriously difficult to verify. You may not be able to remember every detail about an event; your reader might need more detail than you possess in order for the event to be realised. You will have to make decisions as to how self-conscious you are going to be in the way that you admit this. It is important to remember that your version of the past, no matter the imaginative input, will not be just an arbitrary confabulation; it will be grounded in the original experience. Imagination isn't just a whimsical activity, but often a necessary approach taken with material that is sometimes too close, or too distant in time, to see. Imagination is a way of opening up areas of life experience that otherwise would remain shuttered and confined; a way of widening the perspective we have on our own lives. This can be true with biographical subjects too.

## Activity 7.5   Writing

Find a photograph of a character about whom you wish to write, someone other than yourself:

- Describe in your notebook the content of the photo (use up to 50 words).
- Then, again in your notebook, describe as much as you can of that which sits outside of the photo: who was taking it, what was just out of shot, who was present, the location, the time and other such details – some of which may be imagined, some researched (use up to 150 words).
- Now combine and integrate the two versions, so it reads like the story of the photograph being taken (use up to 250 words).

### *Discussion*

This task requires that you ask pragmatic questions about the evidence in front of you. You might not always know definite answers. By doing this you are gauging probability rather than following flights of fancy. The problem often arising when writing from visual stimuli, such as photographs, is that the writer assumes that the reader knows something of the picture already. It's important that you make no assumptions about your reader in this respect. Using photographs can start exciting and unexpected narrative journeys that can explore both autobiographical and biographical subjects – as seen with Mantel and as will shortly be seen in Joan Didion's memoir, *Where I Was From*.

### Research

When writing the previous exercise you might even have found it necessary to do some research and asked someone else questions about details you didn't know. You may have simply checked for a date printed on the back of the photograph. By doing this you are developing the detail in your writing, and enriching the description. As seen in Chapter 2, doing research can be important to your writing. Just because you may be writing about yourself, it doesn't mean you can rest assured that you have all the information you need ready at hand. The corroboration of facts is also an essential part of biographical writing; you will not be able to make certain claims without backing them up.

It might be necessary to locate the precise details about an episode from your own life or the life about which you are writing. This research may involve locating birth and marriage certificates, and other such historical documentation. On occasions it will be a case of looking in reference books and on the internet. Sometimes it will be more to do with contacting and talking to people, or it might even involve revisiting certain locations from your past, as Mantel does, to revive the sensory and emotional recall. The aim in your writing is to build up a substantial picture of events, and to convince your reader of the completeness of this picture. Memory is notoriously full of lacunae, gaps in description and detail. Your ambition, in using research and imagination, is to create as full a picture as possible so that, holes or no holes, the reader is convinced by the complexity of the world you are realising.

### Activity 7.6    Reading

Read the extract below from Joan Didion's *Where I Was From*, where she writes initially about her great-great-great-great-great-grandmother (Elizabeth Scott), then about that grandmother's daughter (Elizabeth Scott Hardin).

In your notebook write down what sort of narrative you think this is and detail the factual elements that have informed Didion's story of her family. What part do you think imagination has played in this narrative?

### from *Where I was From*

Elizabeth Scott was born in 1766, grew up on the Virginia and Carolina frontiers, at age sixteen married an eighteen-year-old veteran of the Revolution and the Cherokee expeditions named Benjamin Hardin IV, moved with him into Tennessee and Kentucky and died on still another frontier, the Oil Trough Bottom on the south bank of the White River in what is now Arkansas but was then Missouri Territory. Elizabeth Scott Hardin was remembered to have hidden in a cave with her children (there were said to have been eleven, only eight of which got recorded) during Indian fighting, and to have been so strong a swimmer that she could ford a river in flood with an infant in her arms. [. . .]

Elizabeth Scott Hardin had bright blue eyes and sick headaches. The White River on which she lived was the same White River on which, a century and a half later, James McDougal would locate his failed White-water development. This is a country at some level not as big as we like to say it is.

I know nothing else about Elizabeth Scott Hardin, but I have her recipe for corn bread, and also for India relish: her granddaughter brought these recipes west in 1846, [. . .] Because that grand-daughter, Nancy Hardin Cornwall, was my great-great-great-grandmother, I have, besides her recipes, a piece of appliqué she made on the crossing. This appliqué, green and red calico on a muslin field, hangs now in my dining room in New York and hung before that in the living room of a house I had on the Pacific Ocean.

(Didion 2003: 3–4)

### Discussion

Although billed 'a memoir' just like Mantel's *Giving up the Ghost*, this extract reads more like a family history, one that leads into national history, detailing as it does the opening up of America's West in the mid-nineteenth century. It spans freely and quickly over a vast historical period, 1766 to the modern day, using family possessions – testimony, recipes and pieces of appliqué – as through-lines to link the various strands. Didion also uses quilts and photographs later in the memoir. All of these artefacts in turn reveal the way of life and attitudes of the various eras. This is one thing that life-writing achieves almost incidentally. When working well it remembers the wider cultural context as well as an individual's situation. With Didion the issues of political and national identity are as prominent the history of the individual identity, if not more so; her memoir amounts to a political and historical memoir of California.

On a personal level Didion's memoir reads fluidly like a tour of family heirlooms; as if all of this information is at Didion's fingertips and she is merely turning like a tour guide from one artefact to the next. The truth is probably rather different, with considerable research and some imaginative venturing, as well as remembering – all of which are hinted at in the narrative. Later, for instance, she uses a photograph as a spur to recall the vocabulary inherited from her grandfather:

A photograph:
A woman standing on a rock in the Sierra Nevada in perhaps 1905.
Actually it is not just a rock but a granite promontory: an igneous outcropping. I use words like 'igneous' and 'outcropping'

**129**

because my grandfather, one of whose mining camps can be seen in the background of this photograph, taught me to use them. He also taught me to distinguish gold-bearing ores from the glittering but worthless serpentine I preferred as a child, an education to no point, since by that time gold was no more worth mining than serpentine and the distinction academic, or possibly wishful.

(Didion 2003: 9)

## Activity 7.7  Writing

Choose an object that has a connection either to your family or a friend. Don't choose a photograph this time, but something that somebody made, gave or wrote. For example, it could be the biscuit tin that is now used to store old Christmas cards, but which originally contained brandy snaps, given to you as a gift by an aunt who once emigrated to Australia with one husband but who came back with another.

In your notebook spend ten minutes listing the associations you have with the object. Then research one further thing about either the object or a person connected to the object. For instance, with the biscuit tin and the travelling aunt, you might ask a relative what happened to the husband she left in Australia; or you might try to find out what year and on what occasion the brandy snaps were given.

Then write the story of the object (use up to 500 words).

## Conclusion

Memory often seems paradoxical – to be both rich and impoverished at the same time. On the one hand there are some memories that come complete with sensory detail. Such scenes can be smelt and touched and heard and tasted, as well as seen. These vivid memories tend to be well rehearsed; they're often thought about; some of them are even talked about and might be shared with others on occasions. The impoverished side of memory appears to be hard to get at, like a locked secret. It can sometimes feel as though you are struggling through the recurring, more vivid memories, trying to get to the rarer ones. Remember Mantel's model of memories laid side by side like seeds in the soil, which runs counter to the more conventional image of memories being buried more deeply the further away they are in time. It is more helpful to see your memories like Mantel suggests – as about to grow into something new.

By actively exploring your memory, asking imaginative questions of 'what really happened' and maybe doing some research, you will be tending the soil, helping your memories to reveal themselves. In this way you will come to learn more about yourself and your subject as you write.

### References

Auster, Paul (1996) *The Red Notebook and Other Writings*, London: Faber & Faber.

Auster, Paul (1988 [1982]) *The Invention of Solitude*, London and Boston: Faber & Faber.

Auster, Paul (2004) *Front Row*, BBC Radio 4, 31 May.

Didion, Joan (2003) *Where I Was From*, London: Flamingo.

Diski, Jenny (1999 [1996]) *The Dream Mistress*, London: Granta.

Diski, Jenny (1998 [1997]) *Skating to Antarctica*, London: Granta.

Diski, Jenny (2004 [2002]) *Stranger on a Train*, London: Virago.

Freud, Sigmund (1955) *The Standard Edition of the Complete Psychological Works of Sigmund Freud Vol. 2: Studies on hysteria*, London: Hogarth Press.

Greene, Graham (1974 [1971]) *A Sort of Life*, Harmondsworth: Penguin.

Hind, Angela (producer) (2005) interview, A215 *Creative Wtiting* CD3, 'Life Writing', Milton Keynes: The Open University/Pier Productions.

Holmes, Richard (2000) *Sidetracks*, London: HarperCollins.

Holroyd, Michael (2002) *Works On Paper: The craft of biography and autobiography*, London: Little, Brown & Co.

Mantel, Hilary (2003) *Giving Up the Ghost: A memoir*, London and New York: Fourth Estate

Piaget, Jean (1951) *Play, Dreams and Imitation in Childhood*, C. Gattegno and F.M. Hodgson (trs.), London: Routledge & Kegan Paul.

Roth, Philip (1988) *The Facts: A novelist's autobiography*, New York: Farrar, Strauss & Giroux.

Salinger, J.D. (1994 [1951]) *Catcher in the Rye*, London: Penguin.

Sartre, Jean-Paul (1963) *Nausea*, Robert Baldick (tr.), Penguin: London. (Original French edition, published in 1938.)

# 8

# Versions of a life

*Derek Neale*

This chapter will elaborate on some of the forms of life writing discussed in Chapter 5, looking at the techniques involved in trying different approaches – such as travel writing, diary writing and dramatic writing. Similarly we will be looking at some of the techniques used in writing fiction that might be of use to the life writer, and we will continue to consider how biographical and autobiographical approaches might sometimes cross over. Although you will ostensibly be dealing in facts and memories based on reality, you will still need to think of how to craft your writing. This chapter will focus on how you might go about producing particular versions of events.

### Writing in diary form

Samuel Pepys's diary was one of the first diaries to be published. It is now regarded as a historical record. It showed a move away from using diaries for business notations towards a more personal type of writing. The most notable modern day form of diary entry is a weblog, sometimes known as a blog, where the private diary entry is circulated via the internet, and can even invite comments and a level of interactivity. In this way blogging is often more than just a private record; blogs can read like testimonies, commentaries, journalism, or even pure fiction. They are conscious of their readership from the start.

Diaries lie on the cusp between private and public worlds. They are a form of writing that can be seen as a personal, secretive dialogue with the self, a form of isolated reflection, or alternatively as a pragmatic exercise in revelation. As mentioned in Chapter 5, diaries are sometimes written purely because of the possibility of publication, as with politicians, whose private and public identities are often under scrutiny. A diary promises insights into the most hidden corners of a character; it offers the potential to reveal a fully fledged identity, one with hopes, doubts, petty preoccupations and grand aspirations.

Sometimes diaries are written as a record of a journey, as with Dervla Murphy's *In Ethiopia with a Mule*, which we will look at shortly. Many writers, like the novelist Elizabeth George, see the writing of a novel as a 'journey' and start a new diary or journal for each new novel. Within the genre of diaries there are different degrees of acknowledgement or awareness that the reader might one day be peering into this private world. Many diaries that make it onto the book shelf are edited and redrafted so their appearance as spontaneous record is as much a question of craft as the well-honed stanza or the succinct short story.

You will shortly be looking at an extract from Anne Frank's diaries. Perhaps contrary to expectation, these diaries, covering a Jewish girl's wartime experiences under the Nazis, were written with a growing awareness of publication. After 1944 Frank started 'rewriting and editing her diary, improving on the text, omitting passages she didn't think were interesting enough and adding others from memory' (Frank 1997 [1947]: v). Before they came to publication, the diaries were also edited by Anne's father, Otto Frank, who chose to omit unflattering descriptions, especially of his dead wife, and details of Anne's nascent sexuality. The problem of censorship is most pertinent to diaries because, as a genre, they are known for revealing salacious detail. These are issues that every writer has to consider. What you might write in your meditative, private diary is not what you might want to reveal to a wider readership. You may well have already used your notebook as a diary, a place of quiet and secure reflection.

We will now explore the possibility of developing and using diary writing as a technique.

## Activity 8.1 Writing

Start a diary for the duration of your work on the next two chapters – or two weeks, whichever is the longer. We will be coming back to this diary at the end of Chapter 9. The important thing is that you start it now; the first entry should be today. For the purposes of this ongoing exercise it would be better if you started a specially designated 'diary', separate from your notebook. This will attempt to be a daily record of your life, though there will be few prescriptions as to form and content.

Make sure you head each entry with at least the date, and possibly the time too (especially if you make more than one entry on any particular day). These entries should be more than a chronicle (a list of events), and more too than a calendar (a list of appointments). Make at least one entry a day. Record anything you wish – but write the first entry before you move on to the next activity. You may wish to record what you've done previously today, who you met with, the weather, your impressions of a person or a place – anything and everything. As a general rule try to keep your entries between 100–200 words.

### Activity 8.2 Reading

Read the following extracts from *The Diary of a Young Girl* by Anne Frank. Note the sort of detail that you think might link the entries together.

#### from *The Day of a Young Girl*

**Monday, 15 June 1942**
I had my birthday party on Sunday afternoon. The Rin Tin Tin film was a big hit with my classmates. I got two brooches, a book-mark and two books.

I'll start by saying a few things about my school and my class, beginning with the other children.

Betty Bloemendaal looks rather poor, and I think she probably is. She lives on an obscure street in West Amsterdam, and none of us knows where it is. She does very well at school, but that's because she works so hard, not because she's clever. She's pretty quiet.

Jacqueline van Maarsen is supposedly my best friend, but I've never had a real friend. At first I thought Jacque would be one, but I was badly mistaken.

D.Q. [Initials have been assigned at random to those persons who prefer to remain anonymous.] is a very nervous girl who's always forgetting things, so the teachers keep giving her extra homework as a punishment. She's very kind, especially to G.Z.

E.S. talks so much it isn't funny. She's always touching your hair or fiddling with your buttons when she asks you something. They say she can't stand me, but I don't care, because I don't like her much either.

Henny Mets is a nice girl with a cheerful disposition, except that she talks in a loud voice and is really childish when we're playing outside. Unfortunately, Henny has a girlfriend named Beppy who's a bad influence on her because she's dirty and vulgar.

J.R. – I could write a whole book about her. J. is a detestable, sneaky, stuck-up, two-faced gossip who thinks she's so grown-up. She's really got Jacque under her spell, and that's a shame. J. is easily offended, bursts into tears at the slightest thing and, to top it all, is a terrible show-off. Miss J. always has to be right. She's very rich, and has a wardrobe full of the most adorable dresses that are much too old for her. She thinks she's gorgeous, but she's not. J. and I can't stand each other.

Ilse Wagner is a nice girl with a cheerful disposition, but she's extremely finicky and can spend hours moaning and groaning about something. Ilse likes me a lot. She's very clever, but lazy.

Hanneli Goslar, or Lies as she's called at school, is a bit on the strange side. She's usually shy – outspoken at home, but reserved with other people. She blabs whatever you tell her to her mother. But she says what she thinks, and lately I've come to appreciate her a great deal.

Nannie van Praag-Sigaar is small, funny and sensible. I think she's nice. She's pretty clever. There isn't much else you can say about Nannie.

Eefje de Jong is, in my opinion, terrific. Though she's only twelve, she's quite the lady. She treats me like a baby. She's also very helpful, and I like her.

G.Z. is the prettiest girl in our class. She has a nice face, but is a bit stupid. I think they're going to hold her back a year, but of course I haven't told her that.

COMMENT ADDED BY ANNE AT A LATER DATE: *To my great surprise, G.Z. wasn't held back a year after all.*

And sitting next to G.Z. is the last of us twelve girls, me. [. . .]

### Saturday, 20 June 1942

Writing in a diary is a really strange experience for someone like me. Not only because I've never written anything before, but also because it seems to me that later on neither I nor anyone else will be interested in the musings of a thirteen-year-old schoolgirl. Oh well, it doesn't matter. I feel like writing, and I have an even greater need to get all kinds of things off my chest.

'Paper has more patience than people.' I thought of this saying on one of those days when I was feeling a little depressed and was sitting at home with my chin in my hands, bored and listless, wondering whether to stay in or go out. I finally stayed where I was, brooding. Yes, paper *does* have more patience, and since I'm not planning to let anyone else read this stiff-backed notebook grandly referred to as a 'diary', unless I should ever find a real friend, it probably won't make a bit of difference.

Now I'm back to the point that prompted me to keep a diary in the first place; I don't have a friend.

Let me put it more clearly, since no one will believe that a thirteen-year-old girl is completely alone in the world. And I'm not. I have loving parents and a sixteen-year-old sister, and there are about thirty people I can call friends. I have a throng of admirers who can't keep their adoring eyes off me and who sometimes have to resort to using a broken pocket mirror to try and catch a glimpse of me in the classroom. I have a family, loving aunts and a good home. No, on the surface I seem to have everything, except my one true friend. All I think about when I'm with friends is having a good time. I can't bring myself to talk about anything but ordinary everyday things. We don't seem to be able to get any closer, and that's the problem. Maybe it's my fault that we don't confide in each other. In any case, that's just how things are, and unfortunately they're not liable to change. This is why I've started the diary.

To enhance the image of this long-awaited friend in my imagination, I don't want to jot down the facts in this diary the way most people would do, but I want the diary to be my friend, and I'm going to call this friend *Kitty*.

(Frank 1997 [1947]: 3–6)

### Discussion

Frank's diary also gives details of all the boys in her class and lists the hardships and oppression suffered by Anne and other Jews in Amsterdam during the Second World War. An intrigue is created by a character who has so many friends yet declares herself friendless. This paradox is amplified by the bleak and terrifying historical situation. Links are made between entries by introducing characters who might then recur. In the first entry you can see an intrigue in the way Frank writes of her supposed best friend, Jaqueline (later referred to as Jaque), failing to elaborate immediately on why Jaque doesn't live up to the title of 'best friend'. Some part of the reason is revealed when Frank writes about J.R., but there is still some detail left out and the reader starts to imagine the relationships between all of the girls. By establishing such characters, Frank, in effect, creates the potential for through-lines, a world and narrative with a sense of continuity, even though each entry is self-contained. As you can see from the last entry in this extract, Frank started to address her diary as 'Kitty' and wrote as if she were writing an informative letter, so engaging the reader as recipient. The reader gets to know Anne's personal attitudes as she writes character sketches, revealing her regard for the people who populate her world. A little after these passages she speculates about who, if anyone, might read 'the musings of a thirteen-year-old schoolgirl', revealing that she is aware of the possibility of a readership and how such writing is strangely positioned between the public and private domains. Note the way in which certain identities are protected by the use of arbitrary initials, as detailed in the footnote on page 3 of the published diary: 'Initials have been assigned at random to those persons who prefer to remain anonymous'. Some of the effect of her editing and 're-visiting' can be seen with such added comments as those about G.Z. This form of reviewing illustrates how personal attitudes to experience can be re-evaluated, and how assessments of situations can change with time and a little reflection.

## There are always different versions

Your perceptions of life events will often alter over time. For instance, at the time you might have seen the dinner with friends the year before last as tedious, but now regard it warmly. This might be because the friends in question have moved away, or because your relationship with them has changed in some other way. Life is always shifting in this fashion, and it has an effect on how you see things. One event will often give rise to many different versions of what happened or what it was like, whether the different perspectives arise from one person over a period or whether they are the views various people hold of the same event. Sometimes the contrast between these different perspectives can be startling. Look at these two versions of the same event:

(a) As the first mushroom floated off into the blue, it changed its shape into a flower-like form – its giant petal curving downward, creamy-white outside, rose-colored inside. It still retained that shape when we gazed at it from a distance of about two hundred miles.

(b) My brother and sisters didn't get to the shelter in time, so they were burnt and crying. Half an hour later my mother appeared. She was covered with blood. She had been making lunch at home when the bomb was dropped. My younger sisters died the next day. My mother – she also died the next day. And then my older brother died.

The event was the dropping of the atomic bomb on Nagasaki, 9 August 1945. The first account, by William Laurence who viewed events through arc-welder's glasses in an 'observer' plane, was published three days after the event in the *New York Times*, and as an 'eye-witness' account was then syndicated worldwide (quoted in Pope 1995: 54–5). The second version, by Fujio Tsujimoto, who was in the playground of his primary school at the time, was gathered through an interview some ten years later (quoted in Pope 1995: 54–5).

You can see from these that the same event has produced not only two different perspectives but also two very different ways of representing that event in language. The first strives almost lyrically to paint a picture of what is happening, yet the identity of the narrator is not apparent. The second creates the family setting and the horrifying personal consequences of the event, and it does so in straightforward language, an edited interview, that produces a chillingly factual effect.

Exploring and detailing different perspectives of the same event can contribute a richness and complexity to your life writing. Yet it also presents a technical challenge. There is always a need to orientate your reader through a stable point of view. Rather than switching from your own perspective, if writing of your life for instance, you have to find ways of incorporating other perspectives while maintaining the stability of the narrative's point of view. This can be done in a number of ways:

- By incorporating 'evidence', such as letters, testimony and diary entries, as a way of introducing other voices. This will also give the appearance of objectivity.
- You can dramatise certain scenes which will 'show' different perspectives through the dialogue.
- You can include interviews with people about certain events.
- You can narrate how you investigated and discovered that there was a different perspective of a particular event.

Through using some or all of these methods, and by using research and imagination, you can incorporate different versions of both your own life, when writing autobiography, and that of your subject, when writing biography. This sort of innovative approach is the way to revive and develop interest in your subject matter.

## Author interview

Getting to know all the facts concerning your subject matter can be essential in order to write about it, but there is also a synthesis involving the research. Such searched for and found material is often not included wholesale in a narrative. Here is another part of my interview with Jenny Diski (seen in the last chapter). As you read, note Diski's approach to research.

Derek Neale (DN): You mentioned that you do as much research for your novels as for your life writing, but with *Skating to Antarctica*, for instance – you include passages about Shackleton; did that come as a result of the journey or did you do that before the journey?

Jenny Diski (JD): Well, I did an awful lot of reading around, I do vague and general and connected reading. When I'm on the journey I read and then when I come back I probably do more reading, I mean I use hardly any of it but I write endless notes on what I've read and then I hardly ever refer back to the notes. So you have to do the notes, you have to do the research and then you have to use, I think, probably as little as you can get away with. I think you've got to know an awful lot about what you're writing even if you never specifically [use your knowledge]. I think there's a texture – you write with knowledge and it's different from writing with as little knowledge as possible. I think you write as little as possible, but you know as much as possible. But for most of the life writing, Chloe (my daughter) went and did all the official bits. I mean she went and discovered birth certificates and all that, so that's how I knew what my grandfather did, that kind of thing. I've got no family to ask questions of, that was the point; it's a blank slate essentially.

What is interesting here is the fact that Diski suggests that the research has almost to be forgotten to be of use. Its residue is what matters. She also reveals how little a writer – even one who is highly educated and self aware – might know at the outset about their own life and family histories.

Now let's look at an example of how some of the strategies we have looked at are used when approaching a biographical subject.

### Activity 8.3    Reading

Read the following transcript of the start of Richard Holmes's *To The Tempest Given*, a radio play based on the poet Shelley's last days in Italy.
In your notebook, detail:

- what sort of 'evidence' you think is used by Holmes;
- what part you think imagination plays in the writing of this sort of biography.

### from *To the Tempest Given*

*wind, storm and sea*
SHELLEY:

> The breath whose might I have invoked in Song
> Descends on me: my spirit's bark is driven
> Far from the shore, far from the trembling throng
> Whose sails were never to the Tempest given;
> The massy earth and sphéred skies are riven!
> I am born darkly, fearfully afar . . .

*fades to seaside, gulls, modern children on holiday*

HOLMES: . . . Yes, my 'spirit's bark.' Shelley always loved boats. At Eton, at Oxford, on Highgate ponds it was paper boats, at Pisa a skiff. That's what brought him to San Terenzo in April 1822, a sailing holiday really, far away from the crowds, the 'trembling throng.' He rented a beach house, Casa Magni, right at the sea's edge, miles from anywhere. It still exists: seven white-washed arches below, four white-washed rooms above, and a long open balcony directly overlooking the surf: a primitive, magical place. Shelley loved the whole set-up. He had a 24-foot yacht especially built for him at the naval dockyards up the coast at Genoa. Typically it had too much sail and too much ballast: very fast and very unstable. [. . .] Mary was with him; and various friends and children packed into the four inhabitable rooms of the Casa Magni. From the various accounts they have left of these last weeks, we can discover a great deal about what was going on, especially from Mary. But it is not always easy to understand at first.

MARY: Our house, Casa Magni, was close to the village of Lerici; the sea came up to the door, a steep wooded hill sheltered it from behind. The proprietor of the estate on which it was situated was insane . . . The scene was of unimaginable beauty. The blue extent of the waters, the almost landlocked bay, the near castle of Lerici shutting it in to the east, and distant Porto Venere to the west, formed a picture such as one sees in Salvator Rosa's landscapes only . . . But sometimes the gales and squalls surrounded the bay with foam, and the sea roared unremittingly, so that we almost fancied ourselves on board a ship.

HOLMES: In reality, what was going on at Casa Magni, below the holiday surface, was very mysterious, very strange. To begin with, a small point, in May and June, one by one all their Italian servants – their cook, their nanny, their odd-job man – left them, saying the place was too remote, too peculiar. Then it became clear that Shelley's wife Mary, who had travelled as happily as a gypsy with him all over Italy for the last four years, was uneasy about this place.

MARY: The sense of misfortune hung over my spirits. No words can tell you how I hated our house and the country about it. Shelley reproached me for this – his health was good and the place quite after his own heart – What could I answer? – No words could describe my feelings – the beauty of the woods made me weep and shudder . . . My only moments of peace were on board that unhappy boat, when lying down with my head on his knees, I shut my eyes and felt the wind and our swift motion alone.

HOLMES: Of course, the biographer has to intervene here and say that we are hearing Mary in retrospect. She may have been the cool, intellectual daughter of the philosopher William Godwin; but she was also a novelist and the author of *Frankenstein*. She was an imaginative woman, and surely her testimony was affected by the appalling series of things that subsequently occurred? Perhaps so: truth is a shimmering, uncertain element, that is refracted through time, like sunlight through shifting water. Yet there is one letter of hers, actually written at this moment, to a friend in Livorno, Leigh Hunt,

(Holmes 2000: 283–5)

### Discussion

Holmes's imagination is prominent here in the way the various testimonies are arranged – those of Percy Bysshe Shelley, Mary Shelley and the other characters. Yet the individual passages seem to be taken from actual letters, journals, poems, and other such testimonies. Holmes himself appears as the master of ceremonies, linking and interpreting all the researched and 'shown' elements. Holmes's interlocutions pursue his subject with a spirit of inquiry and a restless, imaginative approach to the facts, which incidentally aren't confined to what might be learned from books or from the internet. Evidently from his description of the present day Casa Magni, Holmes has done some ground research, as well as reading all the various testimonies. Contrary to what Holroyd suggests about dialogue not being available to the biographer, this docu-drama method allows Holmes to use direct voices and objective summary together with factual 'evidence', so realising different perspectives. We will now consider Holmes's method and approach in more detail.

### Author interview

The biographical narratives of Richard Holmes always contain extensive research of his subject, and in some volumes and biographical pieces he combines this rigorous accumulation of facts with episodes from his own life. On occasions he includes himself in the narrative of his biographical research – as in the radio play you have just looked at. I recorded an interview with Holmes for the Open University and asked him about his approach. As you read the following transcript of the interview, note some answers to the following questions:

- How, when writing about a life, does he balance the need for historical accuracy against the need to tell a story?
- He had already written an exhaustive biography of Shelley when he came to write *To the Tempest Given* – what does he say about why he had to write the play and how he went about it?
- What does he say about the relationship between fiction and life writing?
- What does he mean by 'lost voices'?

Derek Neale (DN): Could you elaborate on your view of biography and how you might go about writing about a subject.

Richard Holmes (RH): There's a kind of fault-line running down between the notion of biography, history, as a kind of fictional retelling and against that the notion that the biographer, the historian must tell the truth, they are committed to the truth, to the facts, to their research. And I would say a lot of my work runs along that fault-line. It's always interested me. Two of the biographies I've written, one about Samuel Taylor Coleridge, the poet, and one about Shelley, the very wild poet, tell the story in a quite traditional way. But I also write books that look at this fault-line between fact and fiction and notably a book called *Footsteps* and this is partly about Robert Louis Stevenson but it's also partly about how I came to know his story and to write about him. And just to set the scene, this all begins when I was 18 years old and I left school and had the sense that I wanted to write and wasn't quite sure what about. So I left England and I went down to France in the Cevennes for about six months and I discovered that young Robert Louis Stevenson had gone down to the Cevennes to make his famous journey with a donkey. What happened was I went up into the Cevennes hills and I followed the route that he made and then years later I tried to write about it. So I was both writing about the young Stevenson and myself as an 18-year-old.

I hitchhiked into Le Monastier which is this little mountain town where Stevenson began his trip and my first conversation is with a certain Monsieur Crèspy who is driving the local van. It's one of those corrugated Citroen vans which has fruit and cheese in the back and Crèspy is not his name, but he did exist. We did have this funny conversation because my French at that point was not very good. One of the central misunderstandings is that I'm trying to explain to Monsieur Crèspy that I'm on the track of Robert Louis Stevenson. Monsieur Crèspy thinks very naturally that [Stevenson] must be a friend of mine who's just a couple of days ahead and I'm trying to explain, no this happened at least 100 years before. In order to point this out I pull out the little book of *Travels with a Donkey* and it's got a map in the front (I love maps incidentally). I try to show Monsieur Crèspy the route and he takes his eyes off the road and we almost drive off the edge of the track.

One extra thing worth saying is that I could remember bits of that early dialogue but when I actually came to write it, details that I hadn't thought about for nearly 20 years came back. For instance there's a little description of the dashboard with a St. Christopher medal and a little cone of flowers. Now those really existed, those flowers, but it was only in writing and trying to describe the inside of the van and Monsieur Crèspy taking his hands off the steering wheel that that came back to me. As you write, as you try and bring back and describe the scene, real things leap back to your pen and you never know what those are going to be and that is part of the absolute continuing magic of it. And now I'm 60 years old, it's just the same. In fact maybe my pen is better than my ordinary memory, if you see what I mean.

I would say for the biographer, you can't normally use dialogue. You can't talk to your subject if they've been dead for 200 years, although sometimes I think you can actually but you can't write it in a book. But what you use is other material, that is to say perhaps their letters or their diaries, or memoirs of accounts of people who did know them and you build that into the story and that takes the place of the novelist's dialogue and through that you do genuinely get the voice of your subject which is one of the important things in biography – to get the voice, to get some physical impression of them.

DN: In much that you write there seems to be an essential combination between journey and writing about a life, In fact when you describe how you came to write about Robert Louis Stevenson you actually went on the journey first and then discovered your subject on the journey.

RH: Yes, I went on the journey without any idea that I would write about him. In terms of writing, my own diary was quite important to me and what I was actually writing was poetry. Diary, travel stuff

**145**

and poetry and only later I realised that the really vivid thing had been my kind of re-imagining Stevenson. It's also true that because I loved writing about the romantic writers, journeying was very important to them. They all made – Byron or Shelley – they all made major journeys which are very important to their writing. Also, I think to understand the physical places in which people lived or grew up or worked, that is tremendously important, to get that physical sense of who they were.

So yes, the journey is important and in *Footsteps* . . . there are various kinds of metaphor that derive from this. One is the broken bridge, because I found one of the bridges that crosses the river that Stevenson writes about. I found the old bridge in a little mountain town called Langogne, very beautiful with a market and everything. But it was broken and they had built a little modern bridge beside it and I couldn't cross over this old bridge. For some reason that became tremendously powerful to me, symbolically. You've got to imagine this rather lonely, solitary, slightly crazed 18-year-old, standing there looking at this bridge thinking 'I can't cross it, so I can't follow Stevenson'. And that for me then became a metaphor – 'Right, you can't really do it so, you know, grow up. You can't really play this game'. But on the other hand, if you start writing about them as a biographer and conform to those rules of historical evidence then you can build your own kind of bridge. In a sense it's about the innocent adolescent view of biography and then gradually learning its rules and trying to grow up within it.

DN: Fiction has plot which often lends it narrative structure and form. Is there an equivalent for biography?

RH: Yes, I think there is. It's tremendously important, but quite difficult to describe. You do have to decide, when you're writing a life, I mean quite simply, what are the most important moments in it, where are you going to spend most time and this is a question of major selection and this would decide the kind of interpretation of the life. For example, is Coleridge's life a comedy or a tragedy? A very simple question but actually quite a profound one and I still, having worked on him for 15 years, wouldn't be able to tell you exactly the answer to that question. But this affects the whole thing, the notion of suspense, what is he trying to achieve in his life? Film-makers talk about a wonderful thing called the hope–dread axis – the thing that you long for and the thing that you most fear. This is true of all storytelling and it's certainly true of biography. What do you hope for your subject and what do you fear for them? The reader should be engaged in that straightaway, I think. In that choice of how you narrate, you are in fact doing something very like traditional plotting.

I'd also say this: in my book *Sidetracks*, I use different types of narrative; for instance there's one story in there which is a biographical essay but it's built like a ghost story. It's about M R James who himself was a ghost writer and each Christmas wrote about a terrible haunting. And the way I write that essay is itself like a ghost story – what really is haunting M R James? There is also a love story which is about the philosopher William Godwin and the feminist Mary Wollstonecraft and I try to tell their story as a couple who met and they definitely didn't fall in love to begin with. In fact they had a tremendous row at their first meeting and then met again about three years later. And then did get married, although neither of them really believed in marriage. But in fact as long as it lasted, it was an amazingly successful marriage and so it's a very interesting kind of love story.

There's another kind of plotting which I call a thriller. For example, there again in *Sidetracks*, I tell the story of someone called Scrope Davies, a wonderful name, who was actually a friend of Byron's and almost forgotten in the Byron story but the story is this. Scrope Davies was a Cambridge don, a clergyman and an obsessional gambler and he had lost an entire fortune whilst still teaching at Cambridge and had to go abroad, had to flee in exile. He left so quickly that he dumped his trunk at his banker's. The story of his life was in this trunk, including all the gambling slips. So, I tell that story and also it gets you out of this very interesting problem with biography. The huge figures, the Byrons, the Shelleys, they exert a kind of astronomical gravitational pressure on stories and they reduce so many people to little tiny moon satellites going round the main story. And often the challenge for the biographer is to turn the little satellite figure into the main figure, to recover their story. It's the notion of recovering lost voices.

There is a wonderful example of this which is a very slim biography that Virginia Woolf wrote and it's called *Flush* and actually it's the biography of Elizabeth Barrett's dog. What Woolf does, she tells the love story, Robert Browning visiting Elizabeth Barrett in Wimpole Street in that terrible kind of parlour she lived in on the chaise longue, in a way as a prisoner, imprisoned by her family, particularly her father. And Robert Browning, the poet, you know it's a famous story, they start by corresponding, and then he comes to visit her and finally they secretly are alone and Flush was genuinely her dog, her companion in that room. Virginia Woolf undertakes to write the love story as seen by the dog, who of course understands no human language, so it's written entirely through smells and the emotions that the dog feels and a kind of ankle-eye view of life and romance.

She does in fact take many details from Elizabeth Barrett's letters because Elizabeth writes very amusingly about the dog. The dog is a sort of comic character in her life. So Woolf actually does have genuine historic sources but there are a set of notes at the end of the book which gives us a glimpse of somebody else in that ménage. This was Elizabeth Barrett's maid, Wilson. In our generation, Margaret Forster has written a wonderful historical novel called *Lady's Maid* which is about Wilson. So that's been passed over, it's like the baton which is passed over from the novelist writing as a biographer on to Margaret Forster, who also writes biography as well as novels, and then it becomes a historical novel. The point of that is the extraordinary exchange that can take place between fact and fiction, but also the central idea of finding the lost voices. After all, Wilson's story is part of an enormous story in that generation, that late Victorian generation, of all the servants, all the women who were governesses, all the maids. What happened to them? Isn't their story very important? Modern biography is very interested by this and so it should be.

DN: This use of genre, is this what you mean when you say that the biographer shouldn't be limited to one kind of narrative voice?

RH: I think there is the traditional biographer's voice, as in the biography of Shelley, although I would also say that you have to find the right biographer's voice for the subject too. In some ways you are mirroring your subject. But, just to follow that through – that biography of Shelley, when I'd finished, I knew there were certain questions I hadn't dealt with which sort of haunted me. One was: what was happening in the last three months of his life when he famously takes the beach hut at the little tiny Tuscan seaside village called San Torenzo, just outside Lerici? The house still exists. I went there, of course, but in those last three months his marriage appears to be breaking down. Yet Mary Shelley is still tremendously important to him. He appears to be having an affair with a friend's wife, Jane Williams, and yet perhaps he isn't. He is writing to Byron and to friends that he can no longer write poetry at all, his career is finished.

Actually he's writing possibly the greatest poem of his life, 'The Triumph of Life'. So there are tremendous contradictions. What's really going on? And I'd narrated it in the biography but I still wanted to know more.

And finally two things happened. When Shelley drowns, which of course he does in his boat, the *Ariel*, he didn't drown alone. He was with his friend Edward Williams, but also with an English boat boy and all that's known about him is his name, Charles Vivian, and probably that he was about 18 or 20 and they'd recruited him I think in Genoa. Nothing else is known about him; he drowns. This is a case of another lost voice and I thought to myself: 'Suppose he'd kept a diary, just like I would have done at 18 – wouldn't it be riveting?' So I wrote Charles Vivian's diary, in a Woolworth's note-book, two volumes, which put down entirely in fictional terms, every-thing that I thought might have happened. When I finished it I thought I can't do anything with this at all, I've broken all the rules; I just can't use it. Yet it still haunted me and finally I thought, yes I think I can use it in a different way. I will play fair, all the voices of Mary Shelley, Shelley, Edward Williams will be from their diaries and letters and poems, but I will invent one character who tells the story, who actually in the radio drama is simply called Holmes the narrator, but who is really Charles Vivian, who sees, who is puzzled, who puts certain questions.

DN: You talk about the biographer having to enter into a dialogue with his or her subject and being haunted?

RH: Yes, I do feel that you need to have that kind of passion about them, but also you have to restrain that in a way. You are trying to be objective, so it's a continual balancing. I sometimes call it love and judgement, but you need that kind of passionate enquiring drive, you're trying to be as objective as you can. It's a balance.

Virginia Woolf used this phrase that biography is a mixture of granite and rainbow and she said that part of the problem is that you have the granite – the facts which you can quarry out – and the bio-grapher has to respect them. But what about the rainbow? Initially she meant by that, I think, the personality. I think she saw a sort of granite building with a rainbow above it. It was a very visual image. It's often interpreted as fact and fiction, that fiction is the rainbow and the gran-ite is the fact. It's not actually what she was saying. It's the personality of the subject that is the rainbow. But I think the most important thing to say is that there is no cheating. If you only set out to write the rainbow you will simply write a bad book or a bad essay. You have to balance the two, you have to respect the granite and be aware of the rainbow. The challenge of the writing is to do those two things, to tell the story, but to be true to the history.

The idea of writing the lost voices – finding and writing about the characters who have not been well recorded by historical record – is a fascinating and inviting project for the biographer. It is a project which will often require the imaginative involvement of the writer, as well as research. It is interesting to compare and contrast Holmes's approach, as declared in this interview, to what Diski says of research in her interview. There are subtle differences, with Diski talking very much from the novelist's corner and Holmes from the biographer's. You will be looking at Holmes' biographical memoir *Footsteps* shortly, to see just how the granite and rainbow are manifest in his own work. First, let's try some biographical writing.

## Activity 8.4   Writing

Pick a celebrity, alive or dead, and research one or two facts about them. Choose someone you are familiar with and about whom you can easily check details. This doesn't mean you have to travel the world – use your existing knowledge, the internet, encyclopaedias and biographical dictionaries.

Write a dialogue between yourself and your subject using these facts. This can be a naturalistic exchange, as if you were meeting them for a drink, or more of a documentary style commentary (as with Holmes), or it could even be an interview with them (use up to 300 words).

## *Discussion*

Each of the suggested methods – naturalistic dialogue, documentary, interview – offers a different benefit. The naturalistic dialogue serves to bring characters to life, as you will see shortly in an extract from Richard Holmes's *Footsteps*. The documentary style allows you, the commentator, to narrate a lot of background information. The interview allows for a little of both, the information being put in the mouth of the subject.

Getting the character to speak in effect creates a docu-drama effect, which is a very familiar form on radio and television.

### Putting yourself in the picture

Sometimes in newspaper or magazine profile articles the interviewer will involve themselves in the narrative of the interview. They will not only ask the questions but also give their impressions of the interviewee's clothes and house, his or her manner, maybe even some personal recollection about the interviewee which lends a more intimate purpose to the article. In effect the writing, though ostensibly biographical, involves itself with two lives, not just one.

A similar relationship between writer and subject can exist in travel writing. As suggested in Chapter 3, this is a form of autobiographical writing which is ostensibly focused on place and therefore less subjective. Yet travelogues like Jenny Diski's *Skating to Antarctica* (1997) and *Stranger on a Train* (2004 [2002]) illustrate how such narratives often concern themselves with people and personal memory. As you will have gathered from the interview with Diski, *Skating to Antarctica* describes a tourist trip to the Antarctic while *Stranger on a Train* describes Diski's travels around the circumference of the USA. Both are interspersed with personal memoir, and interestingly, with the latter, for instance, rather than being full of passing views of America, the features of landscape and place are subsumed by both the characters she meets on her journey and those from her past.

Let's look at a couple of other examples of travel writing.

### Activity 8.5   Reading

Read the extracts from Dervla Murphy's *In Ethiopia with a Mule*, and from Richard Holmes's *Footsteps*, below.

You might like to read the *Footsteps* extract in light of what Holmes says in his interview about how he wrote it. In your notebook, detail the following about both extracts:

- In what way are these about place and travelling?
- What forms of life writing or other techniques do they use?
- In what way do they talk about the author?

## from *In Ethiopia with a Mule*

### 17 December

At lunch-time today I had my first meal of *injara* and *wat*. *Injara* has a bitter taste and a gritty texture; it looks and feels exactly like damp, grey foam-rubber, but is a fermented bread made from *teff*—the cereal grain peculiar to the Ethiopian highlands—and cooked in sheets about half-an-inch thick and two feet in circumference. These are double-folded and served beside one's plate of *wat*—a highly spiced stew of meat or chicken. One eats with the right hand (only), by mopping up the *wat* with the *injara*; and, as in Muslim countries, a servant pours water over one's hands before and after each meal.

During the afternoon a blessed silence enfolds sun-stricken Massawah and I slept soundly from two to five. By then it was a little less hellish outside, so I set forth to see the sights—not that there are many to see here. Visitors are forbidden to enter the grounds of the Imperial Palace and women are forbidden to enter the mosques—of which there are several, though only the new Grand Mosque looks interesting. It was built by the Emperor, presumably to placate his rebellious Eritrean Muslim subjects. In the old city, south of the port, the architecture is pure Arabic, though many of the present population have migrated from the highlands. The narrow streets of solid stone or brick houses seem full of ancient mystery and maimed beggars drag themselves through the dust while diseased dogs slink away at one's approach, looking as though they wanted to snarl but hadn't enough energy left.

### 18 December. Nefasit

The process of converting a cyclist into a hiker is being rather painful. Today I only walked eighteen miles, yet now I feel more tired than if I had cycled a hundred and eighteen; but this is perhaps understandable, as I'm out of training and was carrying fifty pounds from 3,000 to 6,000 feet. At the moment my shoulder muscles are fiery with pain and—despite the most comfortable of boots—three massive blisters are throbbing on each foot.

(Murphy 1968: 11–12)

### from *Footsteps: Adventures of a Romantic Biographer*

I was eighteen.

I had started a travel-diary, teaching myself to write, and trying to find out what was happening to me, what I was feeling. I kept it simple:

> Found a wide soft dry ditch under thorn hedge between the track and the little Loire. Here lit candle once more, studied ground for red ants, then set out bed-roll with all spare clothes between me and my waterproof cloak-sheet. Soon I was gazing up at stars, thinking of all the beats and tramps and travellers *à la belle étoile* from RLS to JK. Story of snakes that are drawn to body-heat and slide into your sleeping-bag. Cicadas and strange sounds river makes at night flowing over rocks. Slept fitfully but without disturbance from man or beast, except a spider in my ear. Saw a green glow-worm like a spark.

I woke at 5 a.m. in a glowing mist, my green sleeping-bag blackened with the dew, for the whole plateau of the Velay is above two thousand feet. I made a fire with twigs gathered the night before, and set water to boil for coffee, in a *petit pois* tin with wire twisted round it as a handle. Then I went down to the Loire, here little more than a stream, and sat naked in a pool cleaning my teeth. Behind me the sun came out and the woodfire smoke turned blue. I felt rapturous and slightly mad.

I reached Le Monastier two hours later, in the local grocer's van, one of those square Citroëns like a corrugated garden privy, which smelt of camembert and apples. Monsieur Crèspy, chauffeur and patron, examined my pack and soaking bag as we jounced along through rolling uplands. Our conversation took place in a sort of no-man's land of irregular French. M. Crèspy's patois and Midi twang battled for meaning against my stonewall classroom phrases. After initial skirmishing, he adopted a firm line of attack.

'You are walking on foot?' he said, leaning back into the depths of the van with one arm and presenting me with a huge yellow pear.

'Yes, yes. I am searching for *un Ecossais*, a Scotsman, a writer, who walked on foot through all this beautiful country.'

'He is a friend of yours? You have lost him?' enquired M. Crèspy with a little frown.

(Holmes 1995: 13–14)

## Discussion

Dervla Murphy's narrative, about a walking expedition to the highlands of Ethiopia in 1966–67, is presented as a journal, headed by dates and punctuated regularly with the details of place and sometimes by times, so the itinerary of the journey is laid out and always given prominence, as is the emotional and physical state of the traveller. Direct speech isn't used as it is in *Footsteps*; rather the narrative gives the writer's first impression of local customs and landscape. It is a more conventional travel format, but allows for occasional elaboration within the text. For instance, it gives information about numbers of American troops stationed in Ethiopia, information that the naïve traveller wouldn't have readily to hand. It also gives more researched information about certain aspects of the journey, and offers regular footnotes about the history of Missawah and the other places visited by Murphy. These are what could be considered to be the conventions of academic writing, often used in biographical writing, and here revealing Murphy's extensive pre- and post-journey research.

Though not included in these extracts, both the Holmes and the Murphy books contain travel writing's common accompaniments – maps of the journey and occasional photographs. The Holmes extract will be familiar from his interview (earlier in this chapter), where he describes the incident he is writing about here. You can see that it is more than just the narrative of a journey; it appears to use a number of different approaches. It traces the steps of Robert Louis Stevenson (RLS), and a journey undertaken by Stevenson in France almost a hundred years prior to Holmes's journey. JK refers to Jack Kerouac and the Beat generation's more contemporary (to 1964, when Holmes's journey was undertaken) vogue for travelling and sleeping rough. This has the feel of biography because Holmes is focused on Stevenson, but it is about an autobiographical journey as well, and gives the flavour of the place, specific to era. In this sense it also works as memoir because it is about Holmes at eighteen, his romantic quest and how he aspired to be a writer, even giving a sample from his journal. It 'shows' the exchanges between characters, so using fictional techniques and conventions to 'remember' dialogue and present it verbatim as direct speech, as in the exchange with Monsieur Crèspy.

### Activity 8.6   Writing

Write about a holiday or journey you have taken in the last twelve months – it might be to a foreign destination, or just to the local super-market (use up to 500 words).

Try to research some new facts about the place, give details about the people encountered, and your personal feelings about the location. Try to 'show' these feelings rather than stating them in abstract terms. Also, dramatise part of the scene with dialogue – even though you might not be able to remember what was said.

### *Discussion*

Place is as important to life writing as it is to fiction. As you can readily see in novels and short stories, characters are often best realised through being shown to be involved with their surroundings. This is equally true of 'real' characters. They may be based on actual people but this doesn't mean they will by right spring vividly from the page. You still need to think of how you are representing them, and the elements of craft and technique involved in that representation.

One of the techniques involved in bringing characters to life is to do with dialogue. It is impossible to remember conversational exchanges verbatim even from yesterday, let alone from ten or twenty years ago. Yet the novelistic convention of dramatising exchanges and giving direct speech to characters can invigorate your approach to a subject. Repro-ducing such unmediated voices will convince your reader that what they are reading is real. There are some, however, who would see this as beyond the bounds of true biographical writing. Remember when using the conventions of travel writing that the essential ingredient isn't the exotic location but the engagement with life and people. A trip to the launderette can produce as good a piece of writing as a journey around the world. You will remember from the last chapter, Jenny Diski talked in her interview of writing about her trips to the supermarket. Her advice was that it isn't necessarily the location that is of interest but the writer's interaction with that location. The reader will be engaged only if they feel they are being invited in to see the interactions and habits, thoughts and way of life of the characters on show, often including those of the narrator.

## Diary reprise

In your daily diary entries started in Activity 8.1, try to include some of the methods used so far in this chapter. Remember that you can use fictional techniques to write about factual matters. So you can write down some dialogue to record a character, exchange or relationship. You can use your imagination and you can dramatise events. You can write about little journeys, describe landscapes and cityscapes, particular kinds of food, and cultural observations. The key is to see the everyday from a new angle. You will recall approaches to this from Chapter 1, when considering how best to 'write about what you know.' Natalie Goldberg suggests that the challenge for any writer is to 'learn to write about the ordinary. Give homage to old coffee cups, sparrows, city buses, thin ham sandwiches. Make a list of everything ordinary you can think of. Keep adding to it' (Goldberg 1986: 100). By trying to write about such things you will see them in a new light. Look for the unfamiliar in the familiar; try to treat each day as a journey.

## Mixing fact and fiction

Holmes's willingness to incorporate many different writing techniques – approaches that stretch the boundaries of biography and autobiography – illustrates how the genre of life writing can be enriched, but also how his content demanded that he improvise with form. The mixture of life writing with other forms of writing can often be productive and irresistible. The modern era has produced a wealth of hybrids which mix fiction, memoir and biography, books which fruitfully explore the border between fact and fantasy. For instance, Philip Roth's *The Facts: A novelist's autobiography*, is addressed to Zuckerman, a recurring fictional character from Roth's novels. As the opening of this autobiography acknowledges, autobiography often contains fiction and fiction is often autobiographical. At the end of *The Facts* Zuckerman responds to Roth: 'What you choose to tell in fiction is different from what you're permitted to tell when nothing's being fictionalized . . .' (Roth 1988: 162).

Zuckerman's response to the autobiography amounts to a critique of the 'careful' memoir, which cares too much about people's feelings:

> I just cannot trust you as a memoirist as I trust you as a novelist because, as I've said, to tell what you tell best is forbidden to you by decorous, citizenly, filial conscience. With this book you've tied your hands behind your back and tried to write it with your toes.
>
> (Roth 1988: 169)

The paradox, of course, is that Roth's very method has admitted the fictional aspect of his autobiography; it is a testimony to the interdependence of fiction and life writing. There is deep irony and ambiguity in Roth's title, *The Facts*, because both types of writing, autobiography and fiction, are seen to be multiplying the possibilities about 'what actually happened' rather than pinning them down. You too might find this in your writing. By writing about your experience you can develop a deeper and richer picture of your own life, but one which is no longer simply reduced to a set of facts or straightforward anecdotes.

Often you will find that adhering too rigidly to the facts of your life can be limiting. Finding a fictional aspect on events can revive those events and make them in a strange way more truthful. As you heard in Chapter 1, Jamaica Kincaid suggests 'To say exactly what happened was less than what I knew happened', in explanation of why she writes (autobiographical) fiction as opposed to a more conventional autobiography. This is testimony from a student writer:

> I found that when I started writing entries for the TooWrite [competition], which have to be true, simply writing down 'what happened' didn't work. I had to 'fictionalise' my own life, or at least remove myself from the equation and write as though I was dealing with someone else's story. I still wrote in the first person, but instead of just writing what happened I used symbolism . . . such as a child's tea set, which I used to symbolise the domestic 'bliss' . . . or a front door to symbolise how trapped I felt by the situation at home. In reality, neither the tea set nor the door were that [significant] in my life until I wanted to find a way of getting my stories across.
>
> (Hartshorn 2004)

**157**

As seen in the last chapter, this is similar to what Auster says of using the third person in his autobiographical *The Invention of Solitude*. Notice how prior to writing about the memories, the tea set and the door were of no consequence. In this way these items, though based on fact, were used more like fictional devices, created in order to reveal the true complexity of the situation.

## Inventing other lives

This attitude to life writing – using fiction techniques – can be extended to writing about other lives as well as your own. The sense of 'play' used in the writing of fiction is equally necessary to the writing of biography, and can often invigorate a subject. You will recall that in his interview Richard Holmes drew our attention to Virginia Woolf, who wrote a biography of Elizabeth Barrett Browning's dog, *Flush* (1998 [1933]). This was a book which in one way was a parody of conventional biography and, as Woolf admits, of Lytton Strachey's *Eminent Victorians* (Woolf 1998 [1933]: xvi). Yet by choosing this fictional approach, Woolf succeeded in viewing her subject matter from a unique angle, one which lent her narrative a parallel: the subordinate or lowly viewpoint of the dog was akin to the lowly status of Victorian women poets, or at least how they were viewed in the 1930s when Woolf was writing. As she admits: 'yes, they are much alike, Mrs Browning and her dog' (Woolf 1998 [1933]: xvii).

Julie Myerson's *Home: The story of everyone who ever lived in our house* (2004) is a biography of her own home, and all its former inhabitants. This project called for much research and verges on social history, but is still concerned primarily with lives. In this way the focus of the writing can shift radically when you choose your 'angle' and the range of your subject. Such unusual biographies could be said to have dual subjects, as with *Flush* where the subjects are the dog and Barrett Browning, or even multiple subjects, as with Myerson and the occupants of her house. It can take on even larger proportions if you choose a wider focus, for instance a city, as in Peter Ackroyd's *London: The biography* (2001), which views the city as a human body, and amounts to a vast historical and cultural guidebook. When considering your subject matter and your angle, you should be aware that there are many alternatives. A single person isn't the only option. You might write about a house or a dog, or you could write about a cricket team, or a village, or a street. Life writing potentially treads the path between social history and personal reflection. The important thing is that the writer is motivated with regard to his or her subject.

Philip Roth's ' "I Always Wanted You to Admire My Fasting"; or Looking at Kafka' is interesting in this respect because its chosen angle makes it hard to classify. Written in two parts, it takes the combination of biography, autobiography and fiction to a new level. Its subject is the writer Franz Kafka, and the first part begins with a familiar life writing prop, a picture, and seems to be straightforward biography: 'I am looking, as I write of Kafka, at the photograph taken of him at the age of forty (my age) – it is 1924, as sweet and hopeful a year as he may ever have known as a man, and the year of his death' (Roth 1973: 103). Noticeably the autobiographical first person is also prominent in this opening discussion, which then goes on to speculate about what might have happened had Kafka not died when he did, but instead emigrated to the US. It proceeds with elements of literary criticism, biography, and eulogy, giving many details about Kafka's life and punctuating the narrative regularly with dates. It is a literary hybrid, one on which the generic labels don't stick very easily. It shifts genres altogether in the second part.

### Activity 8.7   Reading

Read the following extract from the second part of Philip Roth's ' "I Always Wanted You to Admire My Fasting"; or Looking at Kafka'. List in your notebook what categories of writing you think it might fall under.

### from ' "I Always Wanted You to Admire My Fasting"; or, Looking at Kafka'

1942. I AM NINE; my Hebrew school teacher, Dr. Kafka, is fifty-nine. To the little boys who must attend his 'four-to-five' class each afternoon, he is known—in part because of his remote and melancholy foreignness, but largely because we vent on him our resentment at having to learn an ancient calligraphy at the very hour we should be out screaming our heads off on the ball-field—he is known as Dr. Kishka. Named, I confess, by me. His sour breath, spiced with intestinal juices by five in the afternoon, makes the Yiddish word for 'insides' particularly telling, I think. Cruel, yes, but in truth I would have cut out my tongue had I ever imagined the name would become legend. A coddled child, I do not yet think of myself as persuasive, nor, quite yet, as a literary force in the world. My jokes don't hurt, how could they, I'm so adorable. And if you don't believe me, just ask my family and the teachers in school. Already at nine, one foot in Harvard, the other in the Catskills. Little Borscht Belt comic that I am outside the classroom, I amuse my friends Schlossman and Ratner on the dark walk home from Hebrew school with an imitation of Kishka, his precise and finicky professorial manner, his German accent, his cough, his gloom. 'Doctor *Kishka!*' cries Schlossman, and hurls himself savagely against the newsstand that belongs to the candy store owner whom Schlossman drives just a little crazier each night. 'Doctor Franz—Doctor Franz—Doctor Franz—*Kishka!*' screams Ratner, and my chubby little friend who lives upstairs from me on nothing but chocolate milk and Mallomars does not stop laughing until, as is his wont (his mother has asked me 'to keep an eye on him' for just this reason), he wets his pants. Schlossman takes the occasion of Ratner's humiliation to pull the little boy's paper out of his notebook and wave it in the air—it is the assignment Dr. Kafka has just returned to us, graded; we were told to make up an alphabet of our own, out of straight lines and curved lines and dots. 'That is all an alphabet is,' he had explained. 'That is all Hebrew is. That is all English is. Straight lines and curved lines and dots.' Ratner's alphabet, for which he received a C, looks like twenty-six skulls strung in a row. I received my A for a curlicued alphabet inspired largely (as Dr. Kafka would seem to have surmised from his comment at the top of the page) by the number eight. Schlossman received an F for forgetting even to do it—and a lot he seems to care, too. He is content—he is *overjoyed*—with things as they are. Just waving a piece of paper in the air, and screaming, '*Kishka! Kishka!*' makes him deliriously happy. We should all be so lucky.

(Roth (1973): 114–15)

## Discussion

This passage would appear to be either an autobiographical account of Roth's schooling or a short story. The fantastical possibility suggested in the first part of the narrative (not seen in this extract) – 'What if the writer Franz Kafka didn't die in 1924, but emigrated to the US?' – has been incorporated as part of the second part of the narrative. Dr Kafka is the narrator's Hebrew teacher and goes on to date his Aunt Rhoda. By using such an imaginative approach – both to the life of Kafka and to his own life – Roth has in effect rejuvenated the genres of biography and memoir, as well as broadening the range of fiction. This mixing of genres is something you might use in your life writing.

### Activity 8.8   Writing

Use the celebrity you wrote about in Activity 8.4. Include this celebrity in a reminiscence about a real incident from your own past. Include some detail about the character's life in your account, as Roth does in 'Looking at Kafka'. (Use up to 350 words.)

### *Discussion*

By writing simultaneously in this biographical, autobiographical and fictional fashion you can find new ways to approach your subject matter. For instance, Roth reveals much about his own character in the way he writes about Kafka. Just by revealing your interest in the celebrity and by the way you write about them, you will be showing a lot to your reader, information which would otherwise take much laborious explanation.

### Conclusion

There are many ways in which lives can be imagined, remembered and investigated – and many ways in which they can be represented. Because elements within a life are 'real' and have a basis in fact, it doesn't mean those elements will automatically be apparent to your reader. By mixing biographical and autobiographical approaches you can sometimes invigorate your subject, so it becomes more than some flat thing to be described. The first person can be included in the narrative about the biographical subject; the third person can equally be used in the autobiographical narrative. Similarly, you can energise your writing through approaching your subject using a well chosen angle, one in which you have a strong interest. This is true whether the subject is your own life or that of someone else. You can dramatise scenes and use the techniques and conventions of other forms of writing, such as the diary, travel writing, academic writing, playwriting and, not least, fiction writing; by doing so you will be giving life to your writing.

## References

Ackroyd, Peter (2001) *London: The biography*, London: Vintage.

Diski, Jenny (1997) *Skating to Antarctica*, London: Granta.

Diski, Jenny (2004 [2002]) *Stranger on a Train*, London: Virago.

Frank, Anne (1997 [1947]) *The Diary of a Young Girl*, Otto H. Frank and Mirjam Pressler (eds), Susan Massotty (tr.), London: Puffin.

Goldberg, Natalie (1986) *Writing Down the Bones: Freeing the writer within*, Boston: Shambhala.

Hartshorn, Tracy (2004) Private email to the Open University's A174 *Start Writing Fiction* tutor group conference.

Hind, Angela (producer) (2005) interviews, A215 *Creative Writing* CD3, 'Life Writing', Milton Keynes: The Open University/Pier Productions.

Holmes, Richard (1995) *Footsteps: Adventures of a romantic biographer*, London: Flamingo.

Holmes, Richard (2000) *Sidetracks: Explorations of a romantic biographer*, London: HarperCollins.

Murphy, Dervla (1968) *In Ethiopia with a Mule*, London: John Murray.

Myerson, Julie (2004) *Home: The story of everyone who ever lived in our house*, London: Flamingo.

Pepys, Samuel (1970–1983) *The Diary of Samuel Pepys*, 11 vols, Robert Latham and William Matthews (eds), London: Bell.

Pope, Rob (1995) *Textual Intervention: Critical and creative strategies for literary studies*, London: Routledge.

Roth, Philip (1973) ' "I Always Wanted You to Admire My Fasting"; or Looking at Kafka', *American Review*, No. 17, May 1973, pp. 103–126.

Roth, Philip (1988) *The Facts: A novelist's autobiography*, New York: Farrar, Straus & Giroux.

Woolf, Virginia (1998 [1933]) *Flush*, Kate Flint (ed.), Oxford: Oxford University Press.

# 9

# Life characters

## *Derek Neale*

Your life story is as much about the people you meet as about you. Life stories are made up of sequences of events, as in a novel, and those events always involve relationships between people. The interest for the reader, as with fiction, lies in the nature of the characters inhabiting a life. As Isaac Bashevis Singer suggests:

> When people come together – let's say they come to a little party or something – you always hear them discuss character. They will say this one had a bad character, this one has a good character, this one is a fool, this one is a miser. Gossip makes the conversation. They all analyse character. It seems that the analysis of character is the highest human entertainment . . . The writers who don't discuss character . . . stop being entertaining.
> (Interview with Richard Burgis 1978, quoted in George 2004: 7–8)

Bashevis Singer's point illuminates the reader's appetite – we like to hear gossip about characters. Life writing's pre-eminent concern with human experience means that it often conjures up a whole raft of characters, both central and peripheral, some drawn at length over time and given great complexity, some painted succinctly in a page or two. It is the complexity of characters' histories and interactions that captivates, enter-tains and lends life writing its story. As with fiction, it is up to the writer to realise character through various techniques, giving characters certain attributes, such as an external appearance, a life history, behaviour, actions, thoughts, and dialogue.

## Diary reprise

Don't forget the ongoing diary which you started in Activity 8.1. You might like to include gossip about characters in your diary. You might also like to include fantastical speculations about the lives of characters that interest you, as Roth does with Kafka. Your thoughts and fantasies can be as relevant and revealing to a potential reader as any material detail. They too are a part of your everyday life.

## Teachers, witches and wild men

Childhood is full of characters who are not fully understood at the time and who can take on mythological status. The frightening, never-seen woman who lives in the 'witch's house' (how many childhoods have a witch's house!); the wild man who sleeps in the park; the mad PE teacher who once ran in a marathon and continually encourages his pupils to try it; the boy in the corner who is late for everything and who is always scruffy. Let's look from a child's perspective at an 'odd' character.

If you look at the following extract from Wole Soyinka's *Aké*, you will see that there are various characters in the scene. Note what elements of characterisation the reader is given. For instance, you might note details about:

- appearance;
- life history;
- behaviour;
- actions;
- thoughts;
- dialogue.

## from *Aké*

One day, a convoy of army trucks stopped by the road, just in front of the row of shops which included ours. Instantly children and women fled in all directions, mothers snatching up their and others' toddlers who happened to be by. The men retreated into shops and doorways and peeped out, prepared for the worst, ready to run or beg for their lives. These were not the regular soldiers who were stationed at Lafenwa barracks. They were the notorious 'Bote', recognizable by their caps. They were said to come from the Congo, and were reputed wild and lawless. People claimed that they descended on shops, took what they needed and left without paying, abducted women and children – raping the former and eating the latter. To call a man Bote became an unpardonable insult; to await their approach was the height of folly.

I was in the shop with Wild Christian who of course had no interest in the Botes' reputation. As every other shop in the vicinity had either shut its doors or been abandoned, they made for ours and asked to purchase the items they required—biscuits, cigarettes, tinned foods, bottled drinks and sweets. I climbed up to take down jars from the shelves, handed them down to Wild Christian. Suddenly I heard a sound which could only be defined as the roar of a dozen outraged lions. Through the space between the soldiers' heads and the top of the wide door I saw the figure of Paa Adatan, his face transfigured by a set, do-or-die expression. He was naked to the waist, his usual bulbous trousers had been pulled up from the calves and tucked into his trouser-band. In one hand I beheld the drawn sword, in the other, a *sẹrẹ* [a mini-gourd with magical powers] into which he muttered, then waved it round in a slow circle before him.

The soldiers turned, stared, and looked at one another.

Wild Christian had heard and recognized the cause of the commotion but was paying it no heed.

Paa Adatan cursed them. 'Bastards! Beasts of no nation! Bote Banza. You no better pass Hitler. Commot for that shop make you fight like men!'

The soldiers did not appear to understand a word, but the gestures could not be mistaken. They whispered among themselves in their strange language, raised their eyebrows and shrugged their shoulders.

(Soyinka 2000 [1981]): 112–113)

*Aké* is a memoir of Soyinka's childhood in Nigeria during the Second World War. In this extract Soyinka remains in the background, but later there are some telling moments that reveal his subordinate, child status, such as when he relishes some sweet biscuits and when he calls a man names, for which he would be slapped 'in other circumstances'.

This extract contains a character who reappears throughout the memoir – Wild Christian, who is given a strong characterisation as a fearsome and fearless shopkeeper and guardian. Yet this episode is more about Paa Adatan. He is a character who patrolled the local area, furious that he could not get into the army, and affronted that he was unable to personally confront Hitler. When he first appears in the scene he has a sword and scabbard, and the reader is given both his regular and his specific appearance – he is bare chested and the trousers he always wears are pulled up from the calves. His behaviour is generally described and then typified as the scene continues. The episode is structured around him: he is introduced, seen in action and then does not die but makes his exit from the narrative. After confronting and being humiliated by the Bote soldiers, he walks off and is never seen by the narrator, Soyinka, again. But before this his general description gives the reader some 'backstory'. So, the portrayal uses some 'showing' (dramatisation) and some 'telling' (narrative summary) – both methods common to the way stories are told in novels.

### Activity 9.1 Writing

Write a scene about a character from your recent or distant past, someone with whom you no longer have dealings. Choose from the following:

- a friend you no longer know;
- an eccentric;
- a shopkeeper;
- a neighbour.

Make sure your scene introduces the character, involves an incident with the character and covers what happened to the character – this could be as simple as 'I never saw him again' as with Soyinka's portrait of Paa Adatan. (Use up to 350 words.)

### Discussion

When creating brief portraits like this, as with Monsieur Crèspy in the *Footsteps* extract, you will usually want to show the character in action.

Dialogue can be part of that action. Showing such exchanges can enhance your main characterisation (yourself if it is autobiographical) and further develop a secondary character, as with Wild Christian in *Aké*.

## Recall and character

Sometimes the recall of characters can be fragmentary; trying to remember more about them can induce digressions, trains of thought that take you away from what you're trying to focus on. In Graham Greene's *A Sort of Life*, for instance:

> My form master in the bottom form was called Frost. Later the school was reorganized and he was put in charge of the preparatory school which occupied a house in which my aunt Maud had once lived – it was there that I first read *Dracula* with great fear one long summer afternoon. The memory is salt with the taste of blood, for I had picked my lip while reading and it wouldn't stop bleeding – I thought I was going to bleed to death, one of Count Dracula's victims.
>
> Frost had the reputation of getting on well with very small boys, but I was a little afraid of him. He used to sweep his black gown around him in a melodramatic gesture, before he indulged his jovial ogrish habit of screwing a fist in one's cheek till it hurt.
>
> (Greene 1974 [1971]: 46–7)

The narrative appears intent on giving the reader details about Greene's schooling but gets wonderfully distracted by a chance sensory and literary association. It still manages to give a fleeting but vivid picture of the character of Frost, who remains a mythic childhood perception, made up of rumour and one or two idiosyncratic mannerisms. Many life characters, not only from childhood, might appear in this archetypal and not-quite-fully-known fashion, as with Paa Adatan, who is not a fully rounded character, more of a fleeting visitor, in Soyinka's narrative. Yet the significance of such characters to the biographical or autobiographical subject can be great.

Also of note in Greene's narrative is the fact that the digressions are all to do with Greene, they aren't arbitrary or irrelevant; all contribute to the book's overall purpose: enlightening the reader about the character of Greene and his life experience. This is the essential through-line that orientates and reassures the reader when detours are taken to such fringe characters. They all link back to the main character's sensibility.

## Activity 9.2   Writing

In your notebook list three teachers or employers that you can remember – they might be characters you liked or disliked. For each one, list some things you can remember about them. You might include:

- your regard for them;
- what they taught or what their job was;
- whether they were good at what they did;
- how they looked, acted, spoke;
- any associations you may have with them, with regard to other particular pupils, other employees or specific incidents.

Now write a brief summary of each (up to 100 words for each character). As this narrative is about you as much as the character, write in the first person and include any relative associations or digressions, but also remember to retain a focus.

### Discussion

This is always a useful exercise when struggling to capture a particular part of your life. You can set yourself the task of finding three or more people from that period and collecting memories about them. For instance, you could do the above activity with any one period of your life – old school friends, old colleagues, former neighbours.

## Writing about your family

Family will inevitably form a large part of any autobiographical writing. Some writers even choose to write not about themselves but about particular family members. This is often the case when the family member is or has been famous, but this isn't the only reason for focusing in this way. For instance, Amos Oz has written a book about his mother (2004), Hanif Kureishi about his father (2004), and Blake Morrison has published books about both his father and his mother (1993, 2002).

As we saw with Anne Frank, when writing about family and friends there is often the need for discretion. You may not want to reveal certain details to the world about particular characters so as not to offend whoever you are writing about, for fear of incurring legal consequences, and because you may wish to keep certain elements of your life, or the life you are writing about, private. For instance, throughout *A Sort of Life*, Greene refers to 'my wife' but never names her and the narrative doesn't venture to give her a character or describe her in any great depth. This is partly to do with the fact that the narrative is concerned more with Greene's early years, but also it is a decision about who should be written about and who should be left out. In certain passages it was unavoidable that Greene's wife be mentioned, yet the level of inclusion was carefully gauged. As seen in the last chapter, another tactic is used by Anne Frank – with some characters who wished to remain anonymous being referred to by non-specific initials. You have also heard how in *Skating to Antarctica* (1997), Jenny Diski changed the names of her childhood neighbours, at their request. As characters they were essential to the narrative of how Diski investigated her childhood, and their inclusion helped realise a period in her past, a particular way of living and thinking. The use of their actual names is of less importance than what they contribute to the narrative.

Now let's look at a characterisation that also reveals much about the relationship between place and people, and the way people thought in a particular era.

### Activity 9.3   Reading

Read the following extract from Lorna Sage's *Bad Blood*. In your notebook, jot down how Grandma is portrayed, with particular regard to geographical, historical and cultural context.

### from *Bad Blood*

Hanmer's pretty mere, the sloping fields that surrounded us, and the hedges overgrown with hawthorn, honeysuckle and dog roses that fringed the lanes, might as well have been a cunning mirage as far as Grandma was concerned. They did nothing to alleviate the lousy desert that made up her picture of village life. She lived like a prisoner, an urban refugee self-immured behind the vicarage's bars and shutters. None of my new school friends were allowed in the house. You could get into the vicarage garden via the side yard, or by climbing over the walls, and that was the way we did it. The whole thing was clandestine, the other children weren't supposed to be really *there* at all, any more than that picturesque backdrop of lake and trees and cows. Meanwhile, insulated and apart, vicarage life went on. In the church, in bars, in books (Grandpa) or in a scented bedroom fug of dreams of home in South Wales (Grandma). That is of Tonypandy in the Rhondda, which rhymed with yonder, but with its Welsh 'd's softened into 'th', so that it seemed the essence of elsewhere.

Her Welsh accent was foreign – sing-song, insidious, unctuous, converting easily to menace. Asthma lent a breathy vehemence to her curses and when she laughed she'd fall into wheezing fits that required a sniff of smelling-salts. She had a repertoire of mysterious private catchphrases that always sent her off. If anyone asked what was the time, she'd retort 'just struck an elephant!' and cackle triumphantly. Then, 'Dew, Dew,' she'd mutter as she got her breath back – or that's what it sounded like – meaning 'Deary me' or 'Well, well', shaking her head. That 'ew' sound was ubiquitous with her. She pronounced 'you' as 'ew', puckering up her small mouth as if to savour the nice or nasty taste you represented.

(Sage 2000: 31)

### Discussion

Grandma is seen here to be a product of place – both Hanmer, an English village bordering North Wales, and the Rhondda valley in South Wales. She is seen as a culturally specific character – the way she speaks, her taste in food (later we learn that rationing made her crave sugar), and 'She shared her Edwardian generation's genteel contempt for sunburn and freckles'. This throws up some intriguing conflicts of class and status in the next generation, as Sage subsequently writes: 'My mother, however, got the worst of both worlds. She inherited the contempt for housework and she was also imbued with the notion that it was a sacred womanly duty' (Sage 2000: 36).

Practically all of Grandma's traits and characteristics are seen to have a cause and quite often also to have a consequence. It is this level of perception and portrayal, together, of course, with the narrator's personal regard for the character that prevents Grandma from being seen as a stereotype.

### Culture and character

In earlier chapters you were invited to think of cultural associations as a way of remembering, and therefore as a source for creating and developing characters and scenarios for stories and poems. The culturally specific elements in *Bad Blood* are not just from one period and place but run across several historical eras, as do the generations of any family. For instance, in another extended portrait in Sage's memoir, that of her best friend, Gail, there is much reference to the popular culture of the 1950s, including film and music. Sage writes of Gail:

> Her eyes shone and she hummed a few bars of Paul Anka's number one hit, 'Diana', about a mythological older woman, which was written when he was fourteen and inspired by falling in love with his babysitter. Against all the odds she'd discovered in Whitchurch a Paul Anka lookalike – same high cheekbones and black, black hair – and although this one's eyes were blue and Paul's were brown (he was 'of Syrian extraction'), they were deep-set and inward-looking in just the right way. He was called Michael Price, a boy like a startled gazelle . . .
>
> (Sage 2000: 214)

Details about the cultural context can reveal much about characters, and such context should not be confined to the performing and popular arts. Revealing what a character reads, for instance, is a peculiarly private disclosure and can show a lot about a character's state of mind at any particular time in their life. Michèle Roberts, for instance, at the age of twelve or so, read stories of the *Knights of King Arthur*, over which she 'wept copiously: Gawain, Tristram, Percival were my heroes. I couldn't bear it when the book revealed that the fellowship of the Round Table came to an end through the involuntary agency of a woman, Guinevere' (Roberts 1983: 104). This conjures up the hopes and ideals of Roberts at a certain age, together with her level of innocence.

Coincidently, Sage writes, like Greene, of reading *Dracula*, but with a slightly different relish. She is talking in the context of how terrifyingly self-conscious and alien she felt in the adolescent world of pop music and boyfriends:

> It was different with books, I still hung on their every word. The

night I finished *Dracula* was a lot more exciting than Saturday night at the Regal. Lying in my private pool of light with moths ricocheting between the bulb and the lampshade, and the wire from the radio aerial tapping on the window, I drifted into a pre-dawn trance while my little brother (not so little any longer, he was nine) slept soundly across the room in the shadows. Although I protested to our parents that I hated having to share a bedroom with Clive, his unconscious presence heightened my pleasure in my orgies of reading. I was sinning with an undead dandy while inno-cents wallowed in oblivion. The night was mine and Dracula's. How I yawned at the thought of common daylight's coffin.

(Sage 2000: 219)

It's important to bear in mind that you don't have to have read *Dracula*, or any particular type of book, for it to be of interest. Sage's enthralment and feeling of alienation are of interest, not necessarily what she is alien-ated by or gravitates towards. You may have felt the reverse, been alienated by books and drawn towards popular music, for instance. *Star Wars*, U2 and *Countdown* will be as enlightening to your reader as Dickens, Woolf and Tolstoy, as long as their significance to the subject of your narrative is fully realised.

By disclosing details of what and how she read, Sage has revealed much of her teenage sensibility, but she does so with an adult's perspec-tive and in a literary fashion. Writing about experience in this manner is very different from some of the immediate, present tense and more deliberately naïve evocations we have looked at. Compare it, for instance, to the Lesley Glaister extract looked at in Chapter 1, which narrates an episode on a beach from a child's perspective. This is a choice you will have to make in your life writing – how much will your narrative be affected by the wisdom and knowledge gained after the event; how much will you try to recreate the original response to the situation.

Compare, for instance, these two narratives of the same events. First, the start of James Joyce's autobiographical novel, *Portrait of the Artist as a Young Man*:

Once upon a time and a very good time it was there was a moocow coming down along the road and this moocow that was coming down along the road met a nicens little boy named baby tuckoo. . . .

His father told him that story: his father looked at him through a glass: he had a hairy face.

He was baby tuckoo.

(Joyce 1977 [1916]: 7)

Second, Anthony Burgess's parody of this in an adult voice:

I remember I would be told infantile stories, altogether appropriate to my infantile station. One of them, I seem to recall, was concerned with a cow coming down the lane – which lane was never specified – and meeting a child who was called (I am embarrassed, inevitably, to recollect this in maturity) some such name as Baby Tuckoo. I myself, apparently, was to be thought of as Baby Tuckoo. Or was it Cuckoo? It is, of course, so long ago . . .

(Burgess 1973: 63)

In Joyce's version we have the childlike words moocow and tuckoo, and naïve, uninterpreted sentences, simulating the child's perspective and world. In Burgess's version there are bigger words and more complicated paragraphs and sentences – though this version noticeably doesn't give the impression of having a more intelligent narrator, in fact quite the opposite. Both reveal gaps in the memory: the first version is written in fragments, like associated memories; the second version explicitly admitting that recall is uncertain. Both reveal very different but equally possible writing approaches to the same subject, which in itself involves a cultural item – a children's story about a cow.

### Activity 9.4    Writing

Recall a book or a film or a television programme or a song or a piece of music. In your notebook, jot down some memories surrounding it and why you liked or disliked it. Don't read it, watch it, or listen to it again to remind yourself – just operate from what you remember. Note:

- when you first came across the item;
- where you lived at the time;
- where you typically were when you were reading, watching, listening;
- if it reminds you of characters from your life;
- if it reminds you of aspirations now gone or still there.

Write up to 150 words about your original reaction to the book, film, programme or music, trying to realise all the things you have just noted; either use some of the diction and language usage you associate with the memory to try to recreate the era or write from the perspective of the present time, with appropriate use of language, acknowledging the vagaries of memory.

### Discussion

Showing what a character reads, watches, or listens to, and where and when they do it, are all great devices for helping you to reveal aspects about your characters' rational and irrational lives, as well as details about their life history. By showing such responses to cultural items you are creating depth in the characterisation. This is effective with biographical subjects as well as when the character is an autobiographical 'I'. Without 'telling' anything about her teenage turmoil, Sage, for instance, 'shows' excitement, fear and delight, just in her regard for one book. Books and popular music can offer exceptionally effective routes back to a particular period in your life, but the absence of such things might also be of significance. Perhaps there were no books on the shelf during your childhood; perhaps there was a piano but no other source of music; perhaps there was no radio or TV. Your cultural life and that of the characters you are writing about will always be of interest to your reader. The language and grammatical formations you choose to portray these characters will also reveal much about your present and past sensibility, and so create a character out of the narrative voice for your reader.

### The heart of the family

In all forms of life writing there are certain characters who feature centrally, they lie at the heart of the narrative. In autobiographical writing one of these characters is obviously going to be the subject – the 'I'. But often in autobiographical writing there are one or more characters who hold almost as much importance as the subject, and upon whom the narrative can often be focused for long stretches. This is evidently the case, for instance, with Blake Morrison's narratives about his parents. Fathers and mothers are a commonly (but not always) used focal point in memoirs, and for a variety of reasons. Sometimes the reasons are to do with a positive regard for the character of the parent; sometimes they are to do with a fierce hatred. Often it is to do with a form of quest in the writer for a better understanding or a yearning to become reconciled to the nature of the writer's relationship with the parent.

Wanting to know a character from your own life better, and to explore that gap between how you see things and how things really are, is a quest commonly and profitably taken up in life writing. This is because it has both an objective and subjective purpose. In writing about one character from the outside you will always be revealing something both to yourself and your readers about who you are. It isn't necessarily estrangement or a difficult relationship with the character you're writing about that will make you want to write about them. Quite often it can be the paradox of their closeness and separateness that prompts the investigation. The need to understand more fully is motivation enough. As you have seen in Chapter 3, a sense of loss through death or absence can also be a strong prompt.

In Tony Harrison's poem 'Long Distance', you can see how the narrator in the poem – Harrison himself – both addresses and portrays a character, and how his regard for the character is revealed. The formal arrangement of this poem is also interesting. What do you make of it?

> Your bed's got two wrong sides. Your life's all grouse.
> I let your phone-call take its dismal course:
>
> *Ah can't stand it no more, this empty house!*
>
> *Carrots choke us wi'out your mam's white sauce!*

Here the poem includes the dialogue of Harrison's father, who misses his wife, Harrison's mother, terribly. Even though she had been dead for two years, the poem declares that Harrison's father still kept her slippers warming and put a hot water bottle in her side of the bed. Later Harrison's father talks of how the joy of eating and drinking has deserted him without his wife, but also because of the onset of diabetes:

> *Ah've allus like things sweet! But now ah push*
> *food down mi throat! Ah'd sooner do wi'out.*
> *And t'only reason now for beer's to flush*
> *(so t'dietician said) mi kidneys out.*
>
> (Harrison 1987 [1984])

**175**

The voice is in Yorkshire dialect and appears on the page to be fragmented by the italics and the use of apostrophes; it is visually divorced from the roman letters of the narrator's voice which starts the poem and which is the dominant voice in the second section – the part in which Harrison reflects on the lives and deaths of both his parents. The poem appears motivated by affection and mourning. The character of his father and the dead mother are portrayed in a realistic fashion. The dialogue and Harrison's voice, together with details of food and lifestyle, offer this sense of reality. The typeface and the stanzas are irregular, revealing the fractures in the family (some of the schisms caused by Harrison's education and achievements as a writer). But the poem is nonetheless bound tightly together, like the loving relationship between mother and father, by the alternate rhyme. The poem is formally bound in other ways as well, countering the apparent fissures. Each section is written in Harrison's longer, sixteen-line version of the sonnet form. In effect they read like elegies – songs of lament – capturing the pathos of old age and death through the magnificence of small detail. The lament grows into a loving celebration of these passing lives.

The form of Harrison's poem, the way it is crafted and arranged, is also part of the content of the poem. It reveals an emotional, though never sentimental, response to his subject matter. And there are other approaches, less traditional in form, as you can see in the following poem by Sharon Olds. What do you notice about the content and form of this poem?

### Parents' Day

I breathed shallow as I looked for her
in the crowd of oncoming parents, I strained
forward, like a gazehound held back on a leash,
then I raced toward her. I remember her being
much bigger than I, her smile of the highest
wattage, a little stiff, sparkling
with consciousness of her prettiness – I
pitied the other girls for having mothers
who looked like mothers, who did not blush.
Sometimes she would have braids around her head like a
goddess or an advertisement for California raisins –
I worshipped her cleanliness, her transfixing

irises, sometimes I thought she could
sense a few genes of hers
dotted here and there in my body
like bits of undissolved sugar
in a recipe that did not quite work out.
For years, when I thought of her, I thought
of the long souring of her life, but on Parents' Day
my heart would band and my lungs swell so I could
feel the tucks and puckers of embroidered
smocking on my chest press into my ribs,
my washboard front vibrate like scraped
tin to see that woman arriving
and to know she was mine.

(Olds 1996)

Olds is, like Harrison, the narrator of a poem about a parent. The poem is focused on her mother and the recurring occasion of parents' evening, rather than one specific occasion. Formally it is very different from Harrison's 'Long Distance'. This poem is written in free verse and portrays the intense affection and pride the poet felt for her mother, hinting at how that regard dissipated in adulthood, but attempting just to rekindle for the moment of the poem some of the details of the mother – the braids and her transfixing irises. The abiding sweetness of the first part of the poem – 'raisins' and 'undissolved sugar' – epitomises Olds's idolisation, and contrasts to the 'souring of her life' in later thoughts.

### Activity 9.5    Writing

Write either a poem (up to sixteen lines) or a reminiscence (up to 250 words) about one of the following:

- someone who is dead who was known to you;
- a well-known person who is dead;
- a person who is no longer known to you.

It should include some details of where and how the person appeared and/or lived.

## *Discussion*

Writing can be a way of reviving characters missing from your current life. By remembering their habits and the objects and mannerisms associated with them it is possible to further your understanding of your relationship with them. In this sort of writing it is especially important to remember that you have a reader, and that you need to balance sentiment and detail. While it is essential that you convey the emotional importance of a particular character, it is also important to avoid mawkishness. Remember that you are seeking to enrich your memory and to enlighten your reader; the quest is for further investigation, further understanding, not to celebrate in a purely nostalgic fashion.

## Author interview

I recorded an interview with Hanif Kureishi for the Open University just after he had published his memoir *My Ear at His Heart: Reading my father* (2004). This is as much a book about the lives of his father and uncle as it is about Kureishi's own life. While you read the transcript of the interview, note the following.

- What is Kureishi's approach to writing about close family?
- Does he regard *My Ear at His Heart* as biography or autobiography?
- What does he say about the differences between fiction and life writing?

Derek Neale (DN): How did you go about writing *My Ear at His Heart*?
Hanif Kureishi (HK): I just thought I'm writing another book, I'm going to read these books written by my father and my uncle and then I'm going to write this book around it. Later on I began to think, 'Oh maybe it's a memoir.' It wasn't an attempt for me to tell the story of my life (which I didn't think was interesting at all). It was an attempt to tell the story of me reading something about my father.
DN: It does actually read like an 'early years' for you. Like a family history.
HK: Yes, there is a certain amount of that. But it's also an investigation of what families are and what families do and the way families live inside you. The messages they pass on to you and how you convert

those into other things. So, it was sort of an investigation into what I was doing as I was doing it, as it were.

DN: You write of your life being inhabited by others, composed of them. Did you use fictional techniques to represent these characters in your memoir? The character of your father say, or your uncle?

HK: When I wrote *My Ear at His Heart* I really tried to keep it down in the sense that I didn't want to fantasise too much around them, I wanted my father to speak through the books that he'd written, my uncle through the books that he'd written, and through my memories of them. You can be completely free when you're writing a novel. You can do anything you like, you can go anywhere, have loads of people in it, all speaking at once, doing lots of things. When I was writing this memoir the point was not to have all this; it was to try and stick to some sort of reality and to find out as much as I could about my father through his words. So writing it was an act of restraint as it were; I didn't want it to be too mad. I've written about my father many times, much more freely in my fiction than I can in a memoir. I mean the point about writing a fiction is that it is a fiction, that you can go anywhere, you can do anything. You are completely free to transform whoever you want into whatever you want.

DN: Memory is a vast resource; it's a big thing isn't it, your life history, your own personal history? Where do you start and how do you find a form for that?

HK: I found these books by my father. That's what I needed. I didn't sit down and think, 'Right, now I'm going to write a memoir of my dad.' I think that would have been a nightmare, because it's as you say, it's a vast ocean, where would you know where to begin, what would you do? But as soon as I'd found these books, these novels written by my father – there were some stories and other material – then suddenly I found a structure; which was there's this boy, he's found this material, he's going to read this material, what does he think about it. So the book really begins with me starting to read these books.

You can see from Kureishi's responses that he perceived the writing as more of a process of biography and it became the story of his own detective work. Though his subjects were members of his own family and very close to him he was still motivated by an investigative urge and the need to understand the constellation of his own relationships. Of interest here is how he purposefully restrained himself and didn't use the fictional techniques that he had previously used when writing his novels. We will now consider how to approach representing the narrator as the main character in the narrative.

## Presenting yourself as the main character

In the narratives looked at over the last three chapters, the autobiographical 'I' has featured sometimes to the fore and sometimes it has taken a back seat. When the character at the front of the stage is the autobiographical 'I', the reader will need to see you more tangibly created as a character in your own right. You may have to give backstory for yourself (as Holmes briefly does for himself in the *Footsteps* extract seen in the last chapter), you may have to give some indication of appearance, give thoughts, and present yourself in action – as if you were presenting a fictional character. You may also wish to give evidence of your point of view, perhaps from a different period of your life. You can do as Holmes does, using his own journal to authenticate his particular state of mind at a particular age and moment in history, or by using other testimony like letters.

## Activity 9.6   Writing

- Read over the diary that you have kept for the past two weeks. Select at least three and no more than five entries that you might use in a narrative of the two weeks. Preferably choose entries with linked elements, i.e. subject matter that recurs.
- Edit these entries into a form that you think would be comprehensible to a reader, by cutting less interesting material and by adding to and correcting other parts.
- Now write a version of your life over the past two weeks, using at least three of these edited diary entries, as illustrative testimony, like Holmes does with his journal extract. Don't forget to portray yourself as a character, perhaps include some backstory, some other characters perhaps, maybe some details of thought and details of what you have read, watched or listened to. (Use up to 750 words.)

### *Discussion*

It is possible to look at all of your diary entries and edit them into some sort of shape. It is more likely though that, as with most writing, there are many entries that would be of use neither to you nor to your reader. Often the chronology of diary entries can help you to form a narrative. This way of juxtaposing narrative elements that aren't necessarily continuous can be similar to the way in which film scenes are 'cut' side by side. So for instance, in a film, you might see the image of a bird flying over woods, then suddenly cut to a hospital bed, then back to the woods. In the diary you can have an entry for Friday when you're happy and writing of a forthcoming trip to the coast, followed by Saturday's entry when you have a headache, and the car breaks down, then Sunday's entry when you've arrived at the coast and the sun is setting over the sea. Diary extracts are of particular use when trying to illustrate the past, and the immediacy of how you felt at a particular moment. Using diaries in this way is a key method of characterisation, either of yourself or your biographical subject.

### Conclusion

Characterisation is as important in life writing as it is in fiction. The reader needs a point of identification with the life that is being written about. The reader wants to know about the complexity of relationships, to have the major characters well drawn and to be able to easily grasp the minor characters. Just as in a short story or novel, the reader needs to learn about motivations, conflicts and thoughts, and to see characters interacting with each other and within their setting. As Bashevis Singer suggests, this is the sort of gossip your reader will be coming to the party for.

Life writing is often compared to portraiture. As Ben Pimlott writes: 'A good biography is like a good portrait: it captures the essence of the sitter by being much more than a likeness. A good portrait is about history, philosophy, milieu. It asks questions as well as answering them, brushstrokes are economical and always to the subtlest effect' (Pimlott 2004: 170).

This spirit of enquiry is essential to life writing, and the subtlety of effect is often achieved by being aware of the possible approaches – the fact that you can use diary techniques or methods from travel and fiction writing, to give just three examples. Writing about a life isn't merely a question of accumulating facts and then spilling them onto the page. It is often a question of asking: 'What most interests me about this life, this moment in a personal history? What is my focus? How can I make it more interesting?' Writing well about a life is a question of art and craft. As Virginia Woolf says, the art of life writing can mix biography and auto-biography, fact and fiction, and can potentially be: '. . . subtle and bold enough to present that queer amalgamation of dream and reality, that perpetual marriage of granite and rainbow' (Woolf 1967 [1925]: 234–5).

## References

Burgess, Anthony (1973) *Joysprick: An introduction to the language of James Joyce*, London: Andre Deutsch.

Diski, Jenny (1997) *Skating to Antarctica*, London: Granta.

George, Elizabeth (2004) *Write Away: One novelist's approach to fiction and the writing life*, London: Hodder & Stoughton.

Greene, Graham (1974 [1971]) *A Sort of Life*, Harmondsworth: Penguin.

Harrison, Tony (1987 [1984]) *Selected Poems*, London: Penguin.

Hind, Angela (producer) (2005) interview, A215 *Creative Wtiting* CD3, 'Life Writing', Milton Keynes: The Open University/Pier Productions.

Joyce, James (1977 [1916]) *Portrait of the Artist as a Young Man*, London: Panther.

Kureishi, Hanif (2004) *My Ear at His Heart*, London: Faber & Faber.

Morrison, Blake (1993) *And When Did You Last See Your Father?*, London: Granta.

Morrison, Blake (2002) *Things My Mother Never Told Me*, London: Chatto and Windus.

Olds, Sharon (1996) *The Wellspring*, London: Jonathan Cape.

Oz, Amos (2004) *A Tale of Love and Darkness*, London: Chatto and Windus.

Pimlott, Ben (2004) 'Brushstrokes' in Bostridge, Mark (ed.), *Lives for Sale: Biographers' tales*, London: Continuum.

Roberts, Michèle (1983) 'Outside My Father's House' in Ursula Owen (ed.), *Fathers: Reflections by daughters*, London: Virago.

Sage, Lorna (2000) *Bad Blood*, London: Fourth Estate.

Soyinka, Wole (2000 [1981])) *Aké: The Years of Childhood*, London: Methuen.

Woolf, Virginia (1967 [1925]) 'The New Biography' in *Collected Essays, Volume Four*, London: Hogarth Press.

# Index

# Related titles from Routledge

## Writing Short Stories
Ailsa Cox

Ideal for those new to the genre or for anyone who wishes to improve their technique, Ailsa Cox's guide will help readers achieve their full potential as a short story writer. The book encourages you to be inventive, to break writing habits and to try something new, by showing the diversity of the short story genre, from cyberpunk to social observation. Each chapter of the book:

- introduces key aspects of the craft of short story writing, including structure, dialogue, characterization, viewpoint, narrative voice and more
- shows how a wide variety of published writers have approached the short story genre, in order to deepen the insights you gain from your own work
- gets you writing, with a series of original, sometimes challenging but always rewarding exercises, which can be tackled alone or adapted for use in a group
- includes activities at the end of each chapter.

Ailsa Cox draws on her experience as a writer to provide essential information on drafting and editing, as well as a rich Resources section, which lists print and online journals that accept the work of new writers. Whether you're writing as part of a course, in a workshop group or at home alone, this book will equip and inspire you to write better short stories, and make you a more skilled, enthusiastic and motivated writer of short stories.

ISBN 13: 978–0–415–30386–6 (hbk)
ISBN 13: 978–0–415–30387–3 (pbk)
ISBN 13: 978–0–203–96262–6 (ebk)

Available at all good bookshops
For ordering and further information please visit
**www.routledgeliterature.com**

# Related titles from Routledge

## Doing Creative Writing
Steve May

What is creative writing? How, and why, is it done?

Creative writing is one of the fastest growing areas of study, essential to disciplines such as English, drama, journalism and media. Aimed at prospective students and those beginning creative writing courses, *Doing Creative Writing* provides the ideal introduction to studying creative writing at university.

This immensely readable book will:

- Equip students for study, summarising what to expect a creative writing course to offer, and so encouraging confidence
- orientate the reader in the field by explaining exactly what is 'done' when we 'do creative writing'
- offer inspirational advice to help get started – and practical advice about how to get the most out of the course as it progresses.

*Doing Creative Writing* draws on the input of students and their views of what they wish they had known before starting creative writing courses, along with the experience of teachers and writers themselves. It also contains a preface by Stephanie Vanderslice demonstrating the global growth of the discipline and the relevance of this book. Steve May's refreshingly clear explanations and advice make this volume essential reading for all those planning to 'do creative writing'.

ISBN 13: 978–0–415–40238–5 (hbk)
ISBN 13: 978–0–415–40239–2 (pbk)
ISBN 13: 978–0–203–93982–6 (ebk)

Available at all good bookshops
For ordering and further information please visit
**www.routledgeliterature.com**

# Related titles from Routledge

## The Routledge Creative Writing Coursebook
### Paul Mills

This step-by-step, practical guide to the process of creative writing provides readers with a comprehensive course in its art and skill. With genre-based chapters, such as life writing, novels and short stories, poetry, fiction for children and screenwriting, it is an indispensable guide to writing successfully. *The Routledge Creative Writing Coursebook*:

- shows new writers how to get started and suggests useful writing habits
- encourages experimentation and creativity
- stimulates critical awareness through discussion of literary theory and a wide range of illustrative texts
- approaches writing as a skill, as well as an art form
- is packed with individual and group exercises
- offers invaluable tips on the revision and editing processes.

Featuring practical suggestions for developing and improving your writing, *The Routledge Creative Writing Coursebook* is an ideal course text for students and an invaluable guide to self-study.

ISBN 13: 978–0–415–31784–9 (hbk)
ISBN 13: 978–0–415–31785–6 (pbk)
ISBN 13: 978–0–203–49901–6 (ebk)

Available at all good bookshops
For ordering and further information please visit
### www.routledgeliterature.com

# Related titles from Routledge

## Creative Writing and the New Humanities
Paul Dawson

'It is rare to have a text that not only meets a very real need academically, but one that is written with heartening persuasion and clarity. This is clearly excellent scholarship.' – *David Morley, Director – University of Warwick Writing Programme*

Discussions about Creative Writing have tended to revolve around the perennial questions 'can writing be taught?' and 'should it be taught?'

In this ambitious new book, Paul Dawson carries the debate far beyond the usual arguments and demonstrates that the discipline of Creative Writing developed as a series of pedagogic responses to the long-standing 'crisis' in literary studies. He traces the emergence of Creative Writing alongside the New Criticism in American universities; examines the writing workshop in relation to theories of creativity and literary criticism; and analyses the evolution of Creative Writing pedagogy alongside and in response to the rise of 'theory' in America, England and Australia.

Paul Dawson's thoroughly researched and engaging book provides a fresh perspective on the importance of Creative Writing to the 'new humanities' and makes a major contribution to current debates about the role of the writer as public intellectual.

ISBN 13: 978–0–415–33220–0 (hbk)
ISBN 13: 978–0–415–33221–7 (pbk)
ISBN 13: 978–0–203–40101–9 (ebk)

Available at all good bookshops
For ordering and further information please visit
**www.routledgeliterature.com**

# Related titles from Routledge

### Playwriting
### A Practical Guide
Noël Greig

'I have spent half my career waiting for this book to be written. Noël Greig is the original great communicator, playwright, mentor, tutor, support, coach and inspiration. His knowledge and ability should be listed as a national asset. Noël's mantra is "only connect" and I have yet to find an individual who has met him, and has failed to do this on a thousand and one levels. Buy this book and prepare to be wowed.' – *Ola Animashawun, Associate Director, Young Writers Programme, The Royal Court Theatre, London.*

What makes a story work?

*Playwriting* offers a practical guide to the creation of text for live performance, and contains a wealth of exercises for all individuals and groups involved in making theatre. It can be used in a range of contexts: either as a step-by-step guide to the creation of an individual play, as a handy resource for a teacher or workshop leader, or as a stimulus for the group-devised play. The result of Noël Greig's thirty years' experience as a playwright, actor, director and teacher, *Playwriting* is the ideal handbook for anyone who engages with playwriting and is ultimately concerned with creating a story and bringing it to life on the stage.

ISBN 13: 978–0–415–31043–7 (hbk)
ISBN 13: 978–0–415–31044–4 (pbk)
ISBN 13: 978–0–203–33497–3 (ebk)

Available at all good bookshops
For ordering and further information please visit
**www.routledgeliterature.com**